PEACE WAS THEIR PROFESSION
SAC: A TRIBUTE

PEACE WAS THEIR PROFESSION
SAC: A TRIBUTE

MIKE HILL, JOHN M. CAMPBELL & DONNA CAMPBELL

Schiffer Military/Aviation History
Atglen, PA

ACKNOWLEDGEMENTS

It took many dedicated individuals to maintain the posture of strength that the Strategic Air Command exhibited during its history. Likewise, it took the dedicated help of many individuals to bring this photographic tribute to completion.

We would like to express our THANKS to the men and women who served in the Strategic Air Command during the entire history of the command, without them there wouldn't be a new feeling of PEACE.

Special Thanks to General Russell Doughtery USAF (ret) for his support and FOREWARD for this project.

Special Thanks must go to T/Sgt John Esser, 5th Bomb Wing PAO. He cut through the red tape and mountains of paperwork to arrange visits to the flightline, and opened many doors that seemed to be stuck.

Special mention to Joe Bruch for opening his collection to our use and for his support.

Thank You to James Crowder PhD, Don Klinko PhD, and Larry Casey from the Tinker AFB History Office for the loan of photos from the archives.

We mention with Thanks, Mr. John Davis of the Kansas Aeronautical Society for his assistance and expertise.

Maj/Gen. James B. Knapp USAF (ret) for his support and loan of photos. Lt/Gen Edgar S. Harris USAF (ret) for his efforts in obtaining photos and for his strong support in this project.

We thank the following for the loan of photos, material and support. Reuben and Hazel Forsberg, Donald Felling, Arthur and Marcia Tunick, Clyde Evely, Tyree Carroll, M/Sgt Sam Evans USAF (ret), Alfred Pietsch, Maj. Dick Starke USAF(ret), Jeff Ethell, Robert Capps, Doug Rued, William Esenhart, Lloyd Stott, Jim Burridge, Ralph Titus, Pete Frizzell, Michael Boss, Thomas R. Taylor, Dan Nash, Leary Johnson, Lt/Col. Michael Moffitt USAF (ret), Thomas Kinchen, E.S. "Woodie" Fraser Jr., James Jenkins, Pat Lewis, Danna Brenner, Jeff McDowall, Brian Rogers, T/Sgt. Kevin Watton USAF, H.D. "Buck"Rigg, Boeing, General Dynamics, M/Sgt. S.D. Hill USAF(ret), Robert Esposito, Steve Link, M/Sgt Elmer Amundson USAF, S/Sgt Jame Frank Jr. USAF.

We would also like to THANK our families for their support and understanding in this endeavor.

Jesse and Jewell Easton
F.D. and Ruth Campbell
Linda, Jason and Jennifer Hill

DEDICATED TO THE MEN, WOMEN AND FAMILIES WHO SERVED AND SUFFERED IN THE STRATEGIC AIR COMMAND.

'WHOM SHALL I SEND AND WHO WILL GO FOR US?"
"HERE AM I ! SEND ME."
(ISIAH 6:8)

In Memory of
Donna F. Campbell
March 1948-May 1994

"She touched our lives with love and kindness."

Book Design by Mary Jane Hannigan

Copyright © 1995 by Mike Hill, John M. Campbell, Donna Campbell.
Library of Congress Catalog Number: 94-66967

Printed in China.
ISBN: 0-88740-688-2

Published by Schiffer Publishing Ltd.
4880 Lower Valley Road
Atglen, PA 19310
Phone: (610) 593-1777; Fax: (610) 593-2002 E-mail: Info@schifferbooks.com
Please visit our web site catalog at www.schifferbooks.com

We are always looking for people to write books on new and related subjects.
If you have an idea for a book, please contact us at the above address.
This book may be purchased from the publisher.
Include $3.95 for shipping. Please try your bookstore first.
You may write for a free catalog.

In Europe, Schiffer books are distributed by:
Bushwood Books
6 Marksbury Ave.
Kew Gardens
Surrey TW9 4JF
England
Phone: 44 (0)208 392-8585 Fax: 44 (0)208 392-9876
E-mail: Info@bushwoodbooks.co.uk
Website: www.bushwoodbooks.co.uk
Free postage in the UK. Europe: air mail at cost.

CONTENTS

Acknowledgements 4
Foreword 7
Introduction 9

Chapter 1: 1940s 10
Chapter 2: 1950s 23
Chapter 3: 1960s 91
Chapter 4: 1970s 143
Chapter 5: 1980s 185
Chapter 6: 1990s 231
Chapter 7: SAC ART 253
Chapter 8: THE FINAL CUT 271
Chapter 9: TIRED IRON 277

Afterword: In Memorium 292

FOREWORD

To all those who share my affection for Strategic Air Command, its people, its mission and its aircraft, a complete collection of photographs of all of the aircraft employed by SAC during its illustrious 45 years is exciting. I am sure that one could, over time, put together some of this – but the authors have done it all for us and I am grateful. We often reflect on SAC's mission and the accomplishment of its people and we focus on its aircraft individually; but here in this splendid photographic history we have the entire inventory on hand to enjoy.

Several years ago, when testifying before the House Armed Services Committee, Chairman Les Aspin asked me what I thought about the experimental (and controversial) Bell/Boeing V-22 Osprey in which the Marine Corps had a high degree of interest for ship to shore utilization. It was not a very pretty aircraft; but, after a moments hesitation, I answered, " Mr. Chairman, I cannot give you an objective appraisal for I have never seen an airplane that I didn't love."

My experience is that, no matter what rank, the service, or flying experience, an aviator looking at a picture of his own aircraft will invariably say, "Wow! isn't she beautiful! – did you ever see a prettier airplane in your life?"

These anecdotal illustrations set the stage for the nostalgic picture trail marked by the authors. Many will not know what all the aircraft portrayed here did - they will not even know their designation; but, they were all used by SAC. Each made a contribution to the deterrent posture that made it possible for SAC's motto to ring true – "PEACE IS OUR PROFESSION."

For those of us who lived everyday of the magnificent 46 year history of SAC, and many of the years preceding its formation, the pictures will pull at heart strings. The turning of every page will generate a watershed of memories and shared experiences. In some instances, it will be bittersweet, in others, it will be glorious - but that is a very accurate part of SAC's history as we lived it.

Mike, John and Donna have demonstrated an unusual sensitivity in collecting these pictures and placing them, carefully in a time frame that is instructive to follow – on generations as well as fascinating to those of us who experienced these events and times. We owe them a debt of gratitude for their tenacity in collecting, analyzing and preserving the pictures that make up this significant publication. It is well done, and done by three individuals who are interested in preserving the legacy of this greatest of all air commands.

SAC will be remembered – and this book will help.

Russell E. Dougherty
General, USAF (Ret)
Arlington Virginia
November 19,1993

INTRODUCTION

Cast your eyes towards the ocean of blue sky above. Watch the clouds for monuments to the warriors of the COLD WAR. If you seek acknowledgement of victory in this conflict, you will watch the sky in vain. To find monuments to these warriors you will have to visit earthly museums scattered across our great nation.

The monuments you will find in these museums are only hulks of once proud and vibrant aircraft. They were alive with the smell of JP-4, hydraulic fluid and human sweat. At times they seemed to be almost a living creature. Each could assume a personality of it's own, sometimes docile, other times, they defied the efforts of the ground crews to "keep them flying."

The Strategic Air Command came to life on March 21,1946 as one of the three major commands in the U.S. Army Air Force. The primary mission was to be able to conduct long range strategic combat operations anywhere in the world. While the basic mission has remained the same, the methods of accomplishing the mission would change dramatically.

From a snail paced beginning in the late-1940s, through the zenith of the 1950s and 1960s, and on towards the final days of the command in the 1990s, those who served lived the motto, PEACE IS OUR PROFESSION. The hours were long, pay was marginal. Yet, there was an intense feeling of pride in the job that had to be done. With the collapse of the Soviet Union, the men and women of the Strategic Air Command became the victors in the cold war.

For forty-six years the mailed fist of the Strategic Air Command stood ready to unleash the most unimaginable array of weapons mankind would ever see. This posture of strength and readiness imposed by the SAC armada convinced any potential aggressor that a nuclear confrontation was not only unwinable, but unthinkable.

Our purpose is not to present a year by year history of the Strategic Air Command. Our purpose is to travel through the forty-six years of SAC in photos. Those who served in SAC will recall that because of the mission, security was always the watchword. With that in mind it is safe to say that SAC has always been camera shy. In spite of the ever present security force, many of the rank and file carried cameras and often took candid shots of the daily grind. Many of the photos in this work are the result of their work along with the work of the official Air Force photographers.

John, Donna and I can only hope that you, the reader, will enjoy our photographic trip down the Strategic Air Command memory lane. This project has been a personal trip down memory lane since I spent my early years as a SAC BRAT. I recall with pride the sense of duty and special commitment that the men and women of the Strategic Air Command displayed.

We hope that you enjoy this photographic tribute to those who served in the pressure cooker environment that was the Strategic Air Command. Their motto, PEACE IS OUR PROFESSION, was never forgotten. Today, the warriors of the cold war can claim another motto, PEACE WAS OUR PRODUCT.

Mike Hill

1
1940s

The second great global conflict had been over for barely six months. The United States was gearing down from a wartime to peacetime mentality. The vast aerial armadas had been retired to the graveyards awaiting the cutters axe. Most who had proudly served, now wore the "ruptured duck" on their lapels showing they had given service to their country in a time of need. Those who had found a home in the Air Force remained to guard the country against any potential foe.

The United States was the only country in the world with the Atomic Bomb and a means to deliver it. The question remained, just how long would we stay number one. Rumor persisted that Soviet Russia was working on their version of the bomb. According to best estimates, it wouldn't be very long before they would have the same nuclear capability.

Strategic Air Command was officially activated on March 21, 1946. The mission handed to this fledgling organization was to be able to conduct long range strategic bombing operations anywhere, any time, on anyone that the situation called for. The new outfit was commanded by General George C. Kenney. General Kenney had won fame in the Pacific during the war by commanding part of the air offensive against Japan. General Kenny and his staff set up the initial headquarters at Bolling Field, Washington D.C.

During the next few months there was a constant shuffle of paper as the staff tried to find out exactly what they had to work with and where they would find the resources to outfit the command. In the beginning, Strategic Air Command listed nine heavy bomb groups, three of which had no aircraft assigned. The 509th Bomb Group was the only group with nuclear weapon experience. With that in mind, the 509th became the cornerstone of SAC. In spite of the paper shuffle that the staff had undertaken, it didn't take long to find out that they really didn't have much to work with, and that the resources they needed were several years down the line.

Roll out of the first B-50 in 1947. The B-50 was an updated B-29 frame. It had a taller tail and used improved R-4360-33 engines.

The 28th Bomb Group took their B-29s from Grand Island Army Air Field, Nebraska to Elmendorf, Alaska in October 1946. This six month TDY was the first group deployment for training. They returned to their new home in Rapid City, South Dakota in April, 1947. (Knapp)

SAC's first operations occurred in July when the 509th Bomb Group dropped the third atomic bomb on Bikini Atoll during Operation "Crossroads." The results were described as good and the 509th returned to its home base at Tucson with another "Mission accomplished."

SAC Headquarters moved to Andrews Field in October and reorganized. The Fifteenth and Eighth Air Forces would remain under operational control of SAC, while the Second Air Force was inactivated and placed under control of the Air Defense Command.

Training missions became the watch word as other units prepared for the unthinkable possibility of a nuclear bombing mission to some distant target. In May 1947, the first maximum effort mission was flown. SAC launched 101 B-29s in a mock bombing-attack against New York City. Results of the mission were terrible. At least thirty aircraft could not get off the ground due to mechanical problems. A second max effort against Los Angeles brought about marginal results.

SAC started to get off the ground with the delivery of the first B-50 in February 1948. The first B-36 was delivered in June, 1948, as were the first air refueling groups. With new aircraft and crews coming in, it appeared that the bomber boys were becoming a force to reckon with.

SAC flexed its muscles when the Soviet Union imposed a blockade around Berlin. While transports flew coal and food during the airlift, SAC sent several groups to forward bases in England as a show of strength if needed.

On October 19, 1948 there was a change in command. General Kenney was relieved by General Curtis E. LeMay. LeMay brought his hard as nails reputation with him along with his own staff. He had commanded the B-29s that defeated Japan in World War II. His first order of business was to move headquarters to Offutt Field near Omaha, Nebraska. After setting up shop in the old Martin bomber plant, LeMay rolled up his sleeves, chomped on his cigar and grabbed his axe to start making changes.

His first move was to see just how good the command was. A maximum effort was flown against Dayton, Ohio. As he expected, not one of the bombers reached the target. To say the least, LeMay was upset over the results. The groups that participated found out in short order that if you valued your career in SAC, the one thing you never wanted to do was upset LeMay.

LeMay knew that for his men to perform as expected, they had to be motivated. Motivation came slow in the form of better housing, spot promotions, and lead crews. It also came in the form of fear. Fear of failure and what that would bring. Spot promotions could be lost if anyone on the crew fouled up. Life in SAC became a pressure cooker, twenty-four hours a day. Screw up and you were on your way to Goose Bay, Labrador. No wing commander ever enjoyed the prospect of a surprise visit from General LeMay. If the prospect of a LeMay visit was frightening, the actual event was absolute hell if the wing wasn't up to snuff. LeMay had his standards, either shape up or ship out.

SAC flexed its arm again and again with record flights by B-29s, B-50s, and the very long range B-36. Although there was improvement in morale, bombing results and combat readiness as the 1940s came to a close, it was apparent that LeMay had inherited a paper SAC.

Strategic Air Command Headquarters building at Andrews Field, Maryland, October 21, 1946. (USAF)

F-51s of SAC's 33rd Fighter Group on the ramp at Roswell Field, September 1947. (USAF)

During 1947 SAC's budget could afford only one designated support unit. The 1st Air Transport Unit operated ten C-54s from Roswell Field, New Mexico. (Joe Bruch Collection)

A 43rd Bomb Group B-29 (44-82234) on the ramp at Davis Monthan Air Force Base, 1947. (Harris)

BM-004 was the first B-36A. She served as a testbed and training aircraft for many SAC crews. (GD)

The 4th Fighter Group was also assigned to SAC for escort duty during 1947. (Author's Collection)

In the beginning SAC's only nuclear capable group was the 509th. They were assigned to fly during Operation Crossroads. (Author's Collection)

On July 1, 1946, DAVE'S DREAM dropped a "Fat Man" type A-Bomb on Bikini Atoll as part of Operation Crossroads. (Author's Collection)

During 1947 SAC had control of two fighter groups flying the F-80A. This F-80 is from the 56th Fighter Group. (USAF)

Loaded with fuel, a KB-29M takes off from Davis Monthan for a refueling sortie in 1948. (Fraser)

A KB-29M from the 43rd crosses the fence at Davis Monthan Air Force Base after a refueling sortie. (Fraser)

During the late 1940s Davis Monthan Field seemed to be the hub of aerial refueling. The base had KB-29s from the 43rd, 68th, 2nd, and 307th Groups. (Fraser)

44-92015, CITY OF FORT WORTH was the first SAC B-36A. She arrived at the 7th Bomb Group on June 26, 1948. (Author's Collection)

The first B-36B was 44-92026 shown here in 7th Bomb Group markings. Her final flight was on July 8, 1948. (Joe Bruch Collection)

A B-36B (44-92032) from the 7th Bomb Group lays down a low level heavy buzz job at Carswell in 1949. (Author's Collection)

Assigned to the 7th Bomb Group in July 1948, 44-92019 served as a training aircraft for combat crews. (USAF)

A B-29A (44-62310) of the 43rd Bomb Group at Davis Monthan Field in late 1947. (Author's Collection)

B-29s from the 28th Bomb Group over the white cliffs of Dover in August 1948 during deployment to RAF Scampton. (28th BW)

Congress investigated the need for the B-36 in order to appropriate funds for the fleet. In an effort to help sway the vote, a flight of B-36s flew over the Capitol to impress those in power. (Joe Bruch Collection)

On September 17, 1947 the Army Air Force became the United States Air Force. Shortly the aircraft of SAC had the new marking painted on the aircraft like this B-29 from the 509th Bomb Group. (Joe Bruch Collection)

SAC's 27th Fighter Escort Group was the first Air Force unit to use the F-82 Twin Mustang. They received their first F-82 in March 1948. (Author's Collection)

OLD FAITHFUL from the 2nd Bomb Group opens the air show at Oslo, Norway September 12, 1948. (Joe Bruch Collection)

Left:
LUCKY LADY II leaves Carswell AFB, Texas on the first non-stop around the world flight. Ninety-four hours and one minute after take-off she landed back at Carswell. (USAF)

Right:
Secretary of the Air Force Stewart Symington greets Captain J. Gallagher and his crew of LUCKY LADY II after their around the world trip, March 2, 1949. (USAF)

Below:
LADY MARY MARGARET V. Note the 15th Air Force Shield and Strategic Air Command on the fuselage. (Author's Collection)

The receiver aircraft trails a small wind sock on a cable while the tanker trails a weighted cable and grappling hook. (Fraser)

The tanker's view of the receiver aircraft as they close the distance trying to snag the trailing cable. (Fraser)

The tanker begins the right to left cross over above and behind the receiver trying to catch the trailing cable. (Fraser)

If all went well, the cross over snagged the cable, which was then reeled into the tanker. (Fraser)

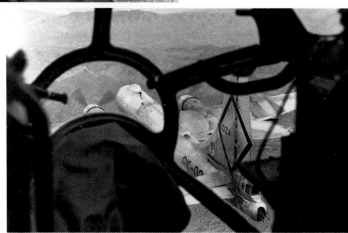

The hose was then reeled back towards the receiver aircraft. (Fraser)

The hose is about ready to be pulled into the refueling receptacle of the B-50 receiver aircraft. (Fraser)

CONTACT! The hose is in the receptacle and fuel will soon be transferred. (Fraser)

Aerial refueling in the early days was a tricky and dangerous undertaking. (Knapp)

At first the fuel flowed by gravity to the receiver, later fuel pumps were installed to aid the transfer through the U-shaped hose. (Fraser)

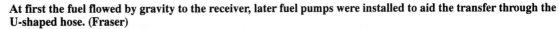

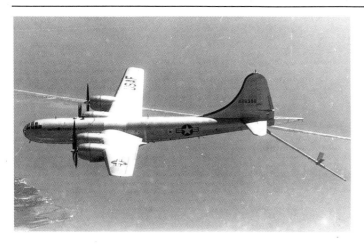

One of six B-29s modified to test the improved engines and fuel injection. 44-86398 was later modified for testing the flying boom concept of aerial refueling and designated as a VCB-29. (USAF)

The prototype KB-29P rolled out of the factory on October 19, 1949. Testing of the "flying boom" began immediately. (Author's Collection)

The concept of aerial refueling to increase range was vital to the global mission of SAC. Here the first boom equipped KB-29P refuels a B-50D. (USAF)

The prototype KB-29P refuels the only B-29 to be modified as a receiver. The 43rd Bomb Group was one of the groups that pioneered the inflight refueling concept using the "flying boom." (USAF)

Sometimes the hose would break causing it to take on the appearance of a huge snake whipping behind the tanker spilling fuel into the slipstream. (Fraser)

HOMOGENIZED ETHYL from the 43rd Air Refueling Squadron. She was deployed to England to refuel the 43rd's B-50s during the 90 day temporary duty (TDY) in 1949. (Joe Bruch)

A trio of Peacemakers fly a hometown formation at low level to impress their escort fighter friends. (Author's Collection)

B-36A (44-92028) thunders off the runway at Carswell AFB, Texas for a training sortie.

The 27th Fighter Escort Group would fly the F-82 until the summer of 1950 when they updated to the F-84E. Author's (Collection)

2
1950s

The 1950s dawned bright and crisp in Omaha. There were new aircraft on the drawing boards. In the first four years SAC had grown from 279 tactical aircraft to over 950. Personnel had been added and judging from re-enlistment records, LeMay's motivation methods were working.

SAC proved that it was ready to meet a challenge anywhere in the world just six months into the new decade. On July 3, 1950, the 22nd and 92nd Bomb Groups received orders to deploy to the far east to help stem North Korean aggression. These units flew SAC's first combat mission on July 13, 1950, hitting the port of Wonson.

In August the 98th and 307th Bomb Groups reinforced the United Nations commitment to Korea. The 98th flew its first combat sortie on August 7th, just five days after leaving Fairchild AFB. The 307th launched its first mission on the 8th, just a week after leaving McDill AFB. It was apparent that the rapid response training was paying off. By September all of the strategic targets had been bombed off the list. SAC recalled the 92nd and 22nd back to the United States. The 98th and 307th would remain to help the United Nation against tactical targets on the Korean peninsula. 1951 saw Korean operations continue with several of SAC's fighter escort groups going overseas to augment Tactical Air Command (TAC).

The first KC-97 aerial tanker was delivered to the 306th Air Refueling Squadron while the first B-47 jet bomber was delivered to the 306th Bomb Wing at McDill on October 23rd. SAC now had

A B-50D refuels from a KB-29P over the snow capped mountains in 1950. (Author's Collection)

MULE TRAIN from the 22nd Bomb Wing is prepared for another trip to the war zone in Korea. (Joe Bruch Collection)

its first real jet strategic bomber. New flying speeds and problems were the name of the game.

To complete its global mission, SAC began rotational training deployments to bases in Japan, Guam and Tripoli. B-36s from the 7th Bomb Wing flew to Lakenheath RAF Station in England while the 11th Bomb Wing took their B-36s to French Morocco.

The third SAC bombing competition was held in August, 1951. This was the first time that a trophy named after General Muir S. Fairchild would be awarded. Known as the Fairchild Trophy, it would become the symbol of excellence in bombing and navigation. The first unit to win the award was the 97th Bomb Wing from the 8th Air Force.

On January 4, 1952 SAC approved an official insignia to start the year off. The design winner was T/Sgt R.T. Barnes from the 92nd Bomb Wing at Fairchild. It featured a mailed fist clutching three lightning bolts for power, and an olive branch for peace.

Combat operations continued in Korea until the formal cease fire declaration on July 27, 1953. During the conflict B-29s from SAC had flown 21, 328 combat effective sorties. It may have been called a "police action", but those who flew the missions knew it had been a real "shootin' war."

SAC tested the combat readiness of the new B-47 with Operation "Sky Try." The 306th Bomb Wing deployed to England for 90 days marking the first overseas deployment of the B-47. When their

TDY (Temporary Duty) time was over they were replaced by B-47s from the 305th Bomb Wing.

In June 1954, B-47s from the 22nd Bomb Wing flew non-stop from March AFB to Yakota Air Base Japan. The 6,700 mile distance was covered in under fifteen hours with the help of air refueling by KC-97s.

B-47s continued to stretch their wings with more record flights and deployments. Operation "Leap Frog" saw B-47s fly from Hunter AFB, Georgia to French Morocco and back in about twenty-five hours. Mid-decade saw SAC increasing rotational training in all areas. There was a constant stream of B-47s and KC-97s crossing the Atlantic or Pacific.

SAC received its new jet-engined "big stick" on June 29, 1955. The 93rd Bomb Wing at Castle AFB, California took delivery of the first B-52 Stratofortress (52-8711). The B-52 was a big aircraft, and the crews that had been selected to fly it could hardly wait to get their chance. When something new arrives, something old usually must go. The last B-50 left the 97th Bomb Wing at Biggs AFB, Texas in October.

F-84Es from the 12th Fighter Escort Wing prepare for deployment to Korea. They were transported on the Navy carrier U.S.S. Sitkoh Bay. (Joe Bruch Collection)

The 27th Fighter Escort Wing bound for Korea aboard the U.S.S. Bataan during November 1950. It took almost two weeks to sail from San Diego to Yokasuka, Japan. (U.S. Navy)

With all the TDYs, operational training and getting the new jet bomber proven, it is easy to see why SAC racked up the first million hours of jet time by 1955. Flying was so intense that an air refueling contact was recorded every three and a half minutes during 1955.

1956 saw two more wings convert to the B-52. The 42nd Bomb Wing at Loring AFB, Maine received their first B-52 in June, and was followed by the 99th Bomb Wing at Westover, Massachusetts in December.

The last B-47 rolled off the production line and was delivered to the 40th Bomb Wing, Schilling AFB, Kansas on October 24th. The Last KC-97 was delivered to the 98th Air Refueling Squadron at Lincoln AFB, Nebraska on November 16th. This brought the full complement of these aircraft on line with SAC.

Changing times and world situations brought about new ideas. In July, SAC announced that it was interested in adding intercontinental missiles to its inventory. It was believed that with new missiles, SAC would have a new and better "Sunday Punch" if needed.

The headquarters staff ushered 1957 in by moving into the new Headquarters Building at Offutt. The building consisted of a three story administration building, with a below ground, three story building that housed the command post. This facility was hardened against anything but a direct hit from a nuclear weapon.

Strained relations with the Soviet Union continued. SAC began to place approximately one third of the bomber force on ground alert. Under Operations "Try Out," "Watch Tower" and "Fresh Start," B-47s and KC-97s perfected the ground alert concept. On October 1, 1957 ground alert operations at several bases within the United States began for real.

Under the concept of ground alert, specific aircraft were parked in a special "alert" area. Loaded with fuel, target folders, secret orders and a nuclear weapon these aircraft could be in the air within fifteen minutes of the klaxon warning.

June 1957 saw the delivery of the first KC-135 jet tanker to the 93rd Air Refueling Squadron at Castle AFB. With this new jet tanker, the bomber could refuel at higher altitudes and safer speeds.

Before the year ended KC-135s were setting world records for that type of aircraft.

As always, new aircraft enter service while older aircraft are retired. In November the first RB-47E was sent to the storage facility. The last KB-29s were also sent to the storage facility in November.

1958 saw reorganization in the ground alert system. Aircrews were moved closer to their aircraft, and from now on they would live within easy travel distance. One more step to get the planes into the air as quickly as possible.

A B-47 from Hunter AFB, Georgia was flying a routine training flight on March 11, 1958. As part of SAC's policy at the time, she was carrying a real bomb in the bomb bay. The nuclear material needed to complete the weapon was stored in the aircraft's safe. During a practice bomb run 200 miles north of Hunter AFB, a bomb lock circuit failed and the bomb dropped from the aircraft. At approximately 4:15 P.M. the bomb exploded with the force of 5,000 pounds of TNT on a farm near Marsbluff, South Carolina. The explosion left a crater seventy five feet across and thirty five feet deep. SAC had suffered its first real "Broken Arrow."

Preparations for a 90 day deployment involved a lot of personal equipment for each crewman. (Harris)

February 22, 1950 the first B-50 and crew from the 2nd Bomb Wing arrived at RAF Marham, England. (Harris)

As part of a reenlistment program SAC adopted the official motto, PEACE IS OUR PROFESSION. It would not only serve as a slogan, it would become the personification of everything SAC stood for.

Based on previous testing, SAC continued working on the airborne alert concept during 1959. This airborne alert system meant that SAC maintained loaded aircraft in the air, twenty-four hours a day, and flew a prescribed pattern on station in the event of an attack. Combined with the policy of 15 minute ground alert, SAC was projecting a posture of power through vigilance to help maintain peace.

In conjunction with the airborne alert, SAC began training for the possibility of using low level penetration techniques to get to the target. Special corridors were set up about twenty miles wide and could run up to 500 miles long. Because of the rapid burning of jet fuel at low altitude these routes were marked by bombers spewing clouds of black smoke as they flew. With this in mind these corridors soon became known as "Oil Burner Routes."

Another program was undertaken to get the aircraft off the ground as quickly as possible. It was found that aircraft could leave the alert pad and undertake a rolling take off on the runway. Each aircraft in the launch cell would begin their take off roll fifteen

seconds after the previous aircraft had started to roll. This meant that there would be several aircraft rolling down the runway at the same time with only fifteen seconds separating them. To say the least, Minimum Interval Take Offs (MITOs) were a sight to behold.

SAC retired the last of the B-36 Peacemakers on February 12, 1959 when B-36, #52-2827, left the 95th Bomb Wing at Biggs AFB, Texas for the storage facility at Davis Monthan AFB.

The decade was ushered out by the eleventh world series of bombing and navigation competition held at McCoy AFB, Florida. Forty seven bomb wings were represented in the October competition. The last BOMBCOMP of the decade was the largest ever held. After a rigorous week of flying and downright cutthroat competition, the 307th Bomb Wing from Lincoln AFB, Nebraska was awarded the Fairchild Trophy.

The first full decade of the Strategic Air Command had seen it grow by leaps and bounds. In 1950 the command mustered just over 85,000 officers and men. At the close of 1959 there were over 262,000 personnel and over 3,200 tactical aircraft. From the slow beginning at the start of the decade, the men and women of the Strategic Air Command now stood ready around the clock to hurl themselves into their cocked aircraft to defend the United States from any aggressor.

Happy to be home after deployment to England. A crew from the 2nd Bomb Wing unloads their gear at Chatham AFB, Georgia in February 1950. (Harris)

B-29s of the 307th Bomb Wing unload on a target somewhere in Korea. (Stott)

It took a lot of fuel to quench the thirst of a B-36. Photo shows 2065 from the 92nd Bomb Wing being serviced in the early 50's. (Author's Collection)

44-92065 was the first B-36B-15 built. She was later updated to B-36D standards and served with the 92nd Bomb Wing during the early 1950s. (Author's Collection)

In February 1950 the 31st Strategic Recon Wing was on TDY to Kadena Air Base, Okinawa. They would still be on station in June when war began in Korea. (Moffitt)

Work continues on a snow covered ramp at Yakota, Japan, 1951. The B-29 is 44-61815, better known as MOON'S MOONBEAM to the 91st Strategic Recon Wing. (Moffitt)

AH SOOOOOO, a RB-29A (44-61817) of the 91st Recon Squadron at Yakota AFB in 1951. (Moffitt)

TIGER LIL of the 91st Strategic Recon Wing heads for a photo target in Korea, 1951. (Moffitt)

Portable shelters cover the engines of the B-50D from the 97th Bomb Wing. SAC ground crews continue the tradition of "keeping them flying" no matter what the weatherman forecasts. (Joe Bruch Collection)

CITY OF ELWOOD, a B-50D from the 509th Bomb Wing. (Joe Bruch)

CITY OF SAN FERNANDO (48-0067) from the 97th Bomb Wing. (Joe Bruch Collection)

B-50D (48-0087) CITY OF CHATTANOOGA, wears the shield of the 97th Bomb Wing. (Joe Bruch Collection)

The 307th Bomb Wing flew its mission on August 8, 1950 just a week after leaving its home base at McDill AFB, Florida. (Stott)

On November 16, 1950 the 91st Strategic Recon Squadron was moved without aircraft of personnel to absorb the assets of the 31st Strategic Recon Squadron at Yakota Air Base Japan. The 31st returned to Travis, AFB, California. (Moffitt)

Three RB-36s from the 5th Strategic Recon Wing fly in the "hometown" formation. The formation was designed to concentrate defensive fire from the B-36's armament. (Moffitt)

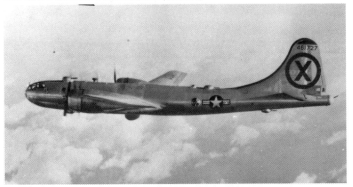

A 91st Strategic Recon Wing RB-29 crosses the coast of Japan headed for a photo mission over Korea. (Moffitt)

The 307th Bomb Wing was one of the three SAC units to remain in service throughout the war in Korea. (Stott)

The first B-36D was 44-92095. The updated aircraft entered service with SAC in late 1950. (GD)

It took a lot of men, equipment, and fuel to keep this 11th Bomb Wing B-36 ready to fly. This B-36 (5734) was one of the stars in the movie Strategic Air Command with Jimmy Stewart and June Allison. (Joe Bruch Collection)

Thule, Greenland 1953. A B-36 from Walker AFB, New Mexico undergoes cold weather testing. (USAF)

A B-36B with updated wings and jet pods from the 7th Bomb Wing, Carswell AFB 1950. (Harris)

A tornado cut a path across the flight line at Carswell on September 1, 1952. The storm damaged seventy-one B-36s. All but one would fly again. (GD)

B-36s from the 92nd Bomb Wing drone through contrail country. (Joe Bruch Collection)

The prototype KC-97 aerial tanker at Boeing Field. The new tanker version of the C-97 will become the backbone of SAC's growing tanker fleet. (Author's Collection)

To move men and equipment, SAC had a total of three support squadrons flying the C-124 like this one photographed on May 15,

By 1950 the 2nd Air Transport Unit had traded their C-54s for the larger and newer C-124 Globemaster. (Joe Bruch Collection)

B-50D (48-0112) served with the 509th Bomb Wing. The 509th used the circle with a red arrow as a marking on the fuel tanks. (Joe Bruch Collection)

A 307th Bomb Wing B-29 on the final bomb run over a Korean target. (Stott)

The 91st Air Refueling Squadron KB-29Ps on the ramp at Castle AFB, California during preparations to deploy for operation Fox Peter One in July 1952. (USAF)

The first KC-97 (51-183) was delivered to the 306th Air Refueling Squadron at McDill AFB, Florida on July 14, 1951. (Author's Collection)

A B-50D from the 97th Bomb Wing taxies out for a training sortie. Practice made perfect as the 97th won the bombing competition, becoming the first unit to win the Fairchild Trophy in 1951. (Joe Bruch Collection)

Cruising above the clouds, a B-47 (51-2071) shows off the clean lines of SAC's new jet bomber. (Author's Collection)

Changing of the guard. A B-47B sits on the ramp while a B-29 sits in the background. A KB-29 flies overhead in this early 1950s photo. (Author's Collection)

Above: The first B-47 (50-008) THE REAL MCCOY was delivered to SAC's 306th Bomb Wing on November 19, 1951. By 1953 SAC had 329 B-47s like this example (51-2363). (USAF)

Right: A sharkmouth B-47B (51-2234) from the 306th Bomb Wing. (Author's Collection)

This RB-36 wears the circle X of the 5th Strategic Recon Wing based at Travis AFB, California during the early 1950s. (Author's Collection)

KC-97 (51-0297) from the 2nd Air Refueling Squadron, 2nd Bomb Wing stationed at Hunter AFB, Georgia 1953. (Harris)

Preflight crew inspection before a training flight. The B-50 and crew are from the 2nd Bomb Wing. Photo taken 1951. (Harris)

KC-97 (52-834) leaves the Boeing plant for delivery to the ever growing fleet of SAC tankers. (Boeing)

A SAC B-50D takes on fuel during early trials with a KC-97. Circa 1951. (Author's Collection)

A thirsty B-47 from the 68th Bomb Wing hangs on the boom of a KC-97. Air refueling between the prop driven tanker and the jet bomber was a "hairy" undertaking. (Fraser)

The 27th Strategic Fighter Wing was deployed to England in May 1955 for ninety day rotational training. Their flight was accomplished by refueling from KC-97s. (Fraser)

A B-47 from the 43rd Bomb Wing left Sisi Slimane, Morocco on November 17, 1954 to return to Fairford RAF Station. Bad weather prevented landing so the B-47 turned back towards Morocco only to find the weather had closed in. With the help of nine refuelings Colonel David Burchinal landed at Fairford after staying in the air for forty-seven hours thirty-five minutes and covering over 21,163 miles. (Joe Bruch Collection)

A KC-97 and a B-47 conducting refueling trials. The ability to refuel bombers transformed the B-47 into a global weapon. (USAF)

A KC-97 from the 306th ARS refuels F-84s from the 31st Strategic Fighter Wing during a practice mission for Operation Longstride. Operation Longstride deployed fighters across the Atlantic on August 20, 1953. (Author's Collection)

High over the Pacific an F-84 from the 31st Fighter Escort Wing moves into position to refuel during Fox Peter One deployment to Misawa, Japan. (USAF)

KB-29Ps from the 91st ARS fly support for Fox Peter Two in October 1953. The seventy-five F-84Gs were led by Col. Donald Blakeslee on the 7800 mile flight from Bergstrom AFB, Texas to Misawa, Japan. (USAF)

F-84Gs from the 27th Fighter Escort Wing on the boom during Fox Peter Two. (USAF)

49th Fighter Wing F-84s refueling from KB-29Ps of the 43rd ARS during a flight from Japan to Bangkok in December 1953. (USAF)

The prototype YRF-84F is about to hook up with the GRB-36 Mothership during trials in 1953.

Hookup completed, the YRF-84 is being hoisted toward the bomb bay of the mothership. (Author's Collection)

KC-97 (51-325) over the pacific during a test hop before assignment to an operation unit. (Boeing)

Fresh from the factory at Wichita this B-47E awaits assignment to a unit. (Author's Collection)

As long as she was flown by the book the B-47 was a good airplane. Miss a chapter and you could end up flying it into the dreaded coffin corner. (Author's Collection)

Dragging the approach chute and power at sixty percent, this B-47 settles in for a landing at McConnell AFB, Kansas. (Author's Collection)

Inches above the runway the pilot of this B-47 can pull the power back and land at McConnell AFB, Kansas. (Author's Collection)

A B-47E (53-2311) on a test flight south of Wichita before assignment to a operational wing. (Boeing)

A B-47E (52-0352) photographed September 4, 1955 at McConnell AFB, Kansas. (Author's Collection)

B-47s of the 22nd Bomb Wing at Yakota, Japan, June 21, 1954. This was the first deployment of the B-47 to Japan. The fifteen hour flight was made possible by two inflight refuelings by KC-97s. (USAF)

Stratojet number 1,000 rolls out of the plant on October 14, 1954. B-47 (52-0609) was delivered to her service unit two months later. (Author's Collection)

B-47E (51-2296) banks toward threatening skies during a training mission in the midwest. (Author's Collection)

B-47 (51-7062) from the 22nd Bomb Wing after the 6,700 mile non-stop flight from March AFB to Yakota AFB, Japan. (USAF)

This B-36B (44-92055) was updated to B-36D standards by adding four J-47 turbojet engines. She carries the markings of the 11th Bomb Wing at Carswell AFB, Texas. (Joe Bruch Collection)

B-36s from the 92nd Bomb Wing thunder into Guam during a deployment December 4, 1954. (Joe Bruch Collection)

A B-36J assigned to the 6th Bomb Wing, Walker AFB, New Mexico. This aircraft has undergone the "featherweight" conversion in this mid-1950s photo. (USAF)

Ground crewman prepare to hoist 126 1,000 pound bombs into this 11th Bomb Wing B-36. (Joe Bruch Collection)

A precarious perch for the two ground crew as they service the nose guns on a RB-36. (USAF)

F-84Fs of the 27th Strategic Fighter Wing on the ramp during Operation Left Hook. This was the first and only SAC fighter competition held in October 1956. The 506th SFW on the event. (Joe Bruch Collection)

Peacemakers, fighters, and snow cover the flight line at Ellsworth AFB, South Dakota. Located on the east edge of the Black Hills it was the home of the 28th Bomb Wing. (Joe Bruch Collection)

The "boomer" on a KC-97 prepares to fly his boom towards the receiver aircraft. (Joe Bruch Collection)

Wearing a red tail, KC-97 (53-0151) sits on the ramp awaiting the next mission. (Author's Collection)

High over Seattle, KC-97 (52-2639) goes through a test flight. Author's Collection)

November 16, 1956, KC-97G (53-3816) was delivered to the 98th Bomb Wing at Lincoln AFB, Nebraska. She was the last of 911 KC-97s built. (Author's Collection)

Ninety day rotation (TDY) of entire wings was made possible by refueling from KC-97s like this one from the 509th ARS. (Fraser)

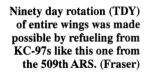

KC-97G (52-0831) leaves the Boeing plant for her operational unit in the mid-1950s. (Felling)

53-2110 one of 386 B-47's built by Lockheed - Marietta. (Author's Collection)

B-47 Jet bomber on alert October, 1956, Guam. On 90-day rotation from March AFB, Calif. (Capps)

A B-47 uses Rocket Assist Take Off to get off the runway at Brize-Norton, England during a 90 day rotation from the 22nd's home base at March AFB, California. (Capps)

Yes Toto, it is Kansas! A winter storm blankets the flight line at Forbes AFB in 1957. (Titus)

The 90th Strat Recon Wing was one of four units using the RB-47. In the summer of 1957 there were approximately 180 RB-47E & H's serving in SAC. (Titus)

RB-47E S/N 52-3379 of the 90th Strat Recon Wing on the snow covered ramp, Forbes AFB, winter 1957. (Titus)

B-52s of the 93rd Bomb Wing on the flightline at castle AFB, California, February 1, 1956. (Ethell)

53 -0388 93rd BW Castle 1956-57.

September 13, 1956, 53-0488 takes off from Loring AFB. (Ethell)

B-52 (58-8710) lands at Eglin AFB, Florida on May 8, 1956 during a test flight. (Ethell)

By February 1956 the 93rd Bomb Wing had only flying practice missions in their new aircraft. (Ethell)

B-52B (52-8716) from the 93rd Bomb Wing. This aircraft crashed on November 30, 1956 killing the crew. (Ethell)

Fresh from the factory 53-6216 heads for her unit and the application of the units markings. (Author's Collection)

Most SAC bomber wings had a sister refueling wing at the same base. During TDY the tankers would deploy first to be in position when the thirsty bombers arrived. (Fraser)

The 91st Strategic Recon Wing sent this RB-45 to Walker AFB, New Mexico in the mid-1950s for these cadets to inspect. (Joe Bruch Collection)

An RF-84K from the 91st Strategic Recon Squadron at Larson AFB, Washington. The squadron was operational during 1955. (Author's Collection)

The crew of RB-36 #750 from the 28th Recon Wing are greeted by their families on return from a ninety day TDY to Guam in 1955. (28th BW)

Men of the 28th Strategic Recon Wing stand in review at Ellsworth AFB while RB-36 #725 provides the backdrop. (28th BW)

SAC's aerial armada would never get off the ground without countless hours spent by the ground crews to keep the planes combat ready and safe to fly. Mechanics from the 5th Strategic Recon Wing labor over a Wright R-3360 engine on this RB-36. (5th BW)

An RB-36 crew from the 5th Strategic Recon Wing based at Travis AFB, June 1956. Two years later the 5th traded their B-36s for the first B-52Gs to reach SAC. (5th BW)

General LeMay prepares to decorate the crews of Operation Powerflight, after their around the world flight. (Joe Bruch Collection)

General Curtis LeMay, now Vice Chief of Staff, flew this KC-135(55-3126) 6,322.85 miles to set a non stop, non refueled distance record on November 11-12, 1957. (Joe Bruch Collection)

B-36 F of 6th BW(H) Walker AFB New Mexico fly formation over SW USA 1956. (USAF)

To help dedicate the Air Force Academy on July 11, 1955, this RB-36F was part of a nine ship formation. About twenty miles from Lowery AFB at about 1,000 feet the entire 32 foot rudder tore away. In spite of the loss of rudder, UHF, and command radio, Major William Deyer and his crew flew the aircraft through a weather front and landed at Ellsworth AFB, South Dakota two and a half hours after the incident. (Felling)

RB-36F (49-2709) on the flightline at Fairchild AFB, Washington, March 25, 1955. (Moffitt)

RB-36F (49-2718) of the 99th SRW at Fairchild AFB, Washington in late 1950's. Plain Jane markings. (Moffitt)

The B-36 had a good safety record. Accidents did happen, like this RB-36 (51-13720). On November 16, 1956 she crashed about a mile short of the runway at Stapleton Airport near Denver. (USAF)

On March 13, 1958 two B-47's crashed. According to a survivor interview, the wing fell off. Another B-47 crashed on March 21. In April, three more crashed. SAC's primary bomber was falling apart. (Tinker AFB Archives)

Engine specialists work on the J-47 engines of a 320 BW B-47. Like all members of SAC, they worked pressure cooker schedules to keep the planes combat ready. (Joe Bruch Collection)

RB-36s from the 28th Wing on the ramp at Ellsworth AFB, South Dakota. (28th BW)

In January 1957 SAC moved into the new headquarters building at Offatt AFB. Prior to the move SAC had been headquarted in the Glen L. Martin B-29 plant at Offatt. (USAF)

Because the B-36 was being retired, SAC no longer required their escort fighters. By July 1957 these F-84F's of the 27th Strategic Fighter Wing were either turned over to Tactical Air Command or a Reserve Unit. (Joe Bruch Collection)

51-185 the third Production KC-97 on short final in the late 50's. (Author's Collection)

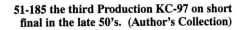

SAC received the first U-2 (56-6696) on June 11, 1957. It was assigned to the 4080th SRW at Laughlin AFB, Texas. (Joe Bruch Collection)

A B-26 invader warms up for a flight. SAC used this aircraft as a trainer and as a support aircraft. (Esposito)

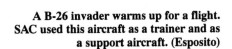

B-52E (56-0631) was the first "E" built. It was delivered to SAC on October 7, 1957. (Ethell)

Operation Power Flight. These three B-52's from the 93rd BW flew around the world non stop January 16-18, 1957. (Ethell)

B-52D (56-0593) from the 99th BW photographed at Pease AFB, October 1957. This aircraft crashed on take off at Anderson AFB, Guam on May 10, 1969 during an Arc Light mission to Viet Nam. (Burridge)

A B-36H (52-1347) from the 7th Bomb Wing takes off from Carswell AFB, Texas. The B-36H had a top speed of 416 mph. (GD)

A Featherweight B-36J takes off for another mission. The Featherweight Peacemakers had all the guns removed except for the tail cannons. (GD)

KC-135A (55-3127) First KC-135 delivered to SAC 93rd ARS Castle, June 28 1957.

Training with the new tanker began at once. A KC-135 refuels a B-52 at altitude.

KC-135 (56-3616) on a training mission. (Ethell)

A KC-135 launches for another mission.

Left: The first Atlas wing was the 4320th SMW at Francis E. Warren AFB, Wyoming. They were activated on February 1, 1958. The designation was changed to the 706th SMW on February 23, 1958. (Joe Bruch Collection)

Below: Three Atlas missles from the 565th SMS stand erect against the Wyoming sky during a launch coordination test. (Joe Bruch Collection)

The 556th SMS launched its first Snark from Patrick AFB, Florida on June 27, 1958.(Joe Bruch Collection)

SAC dispersed their Thor missiles like this one at RAF, Carster, August 1959. (Joe Bruch Collection)

Graduation day of the first class that will man the new Snark missile, December 17, 1957. (Joe Bruch Collection)

56-0692 28th BW starting engines during ORI. (Ethell)

53-0394
93rd BW,
Castle AFB
1957.

December 10, 1958 , 55-0586 taxing back to flightline at Loring after Operation Headstart. (Ethell)

The first B-52G (57-6468) rolled off the line on July 23, 1958.

February 13, 1959, 5th BW Travis AFB accepts first SAC B-52G (57-6478).

B-52D (56-0695), a Quail decoy. After long service, including combat in SEA, she retired in October 1983. She is preserved at the Tinker AFB Heritage Museum. (Ethell)

B-25's were used as utility aircraft as well a bomb/nav trainers.

C-119's were used to haul just about everything SAC needed.

The updated B-50D first flew on May 23, 1949. They began reaching operational units later that year, replacing the B-29 as a front line bomber. (Knapp)

The 91st Strategic Recon Wing received the first RB-45C on August 26, 1950. The RB-45C was the first multi-engine jet aircraft to reach SAC's inventory. (Joe Bruch Collection)

The first TDY of a B-36 wing to an overseas base was carried out by the 92nd Wing at Fairchild AFB. In October 1954 they rotated "lock, stock, and bag" to Anderson AFB, Guam for ninety days. (Felling)

On June 29, 1955 the 93rd Bomb Wing received the first B-52B (52-8711) from Boeing. SAC now had a new big stick jet bomber in the inventory. (Hill)

For a few months in 1949 SAC had control of the 1st Fighter Group at March AFB, California. The 1st Fighter Group at March AFB, California. The 1st was using the new F-86A like this one from the 94th Fighter Squadron of the group. (Author's Collection)

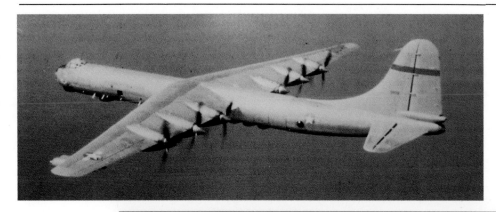

By the mid-1950s B-36 markings had been toned down. Gone were the large tail codes. This RB-36F (50-1110) carries only a red tail stripe and the SAC sash and crest. (Knapp)

This B-36 from the 7th Bomb Group sports a red tail. These markings were used on the B-36s that conducted cold weather trials. (Joe Bruch Collection)

SAC started using the RB-57D in May 1956. Later the 4080th Strategic Recon Wing received the updated RB-57F. (USAF)

The watchword in SAC was, "Don't screw up, they'll send you to Thule." Actually it was an important base. It provided an emergency stopover and tankers for the long Atlantic crossing. (Lewis)

Depending on the season, daylight was either long or non-existent at Thule, Greenland. (Lewis)

KC-97 (53-0140) of the 320th Air Refueling Wing at Thule, Greenland during a ninety day TDY deployment to England in 1955. (Author's Collection)

A KC-97 (53-0297) on the ramp at March AFB, California. (Author's Collection)

High over the Atlantic a KC-97 (51-281) waits for the receiver aircraft to arrive for another aerial refueling. (Knapp)

KC-97 (51-0241) sits on the ramp awaiting her next crew and mission.

Rain hasn't dampened the spirit of the airshow crowd as they inspect a KC-97.(Author's Collection)

"Day-glo" paint was added to the tanker fleet in the late "50's" to increase visibility during rendezvouz. (Johnson)

Wingtip and fuel tank gone, this KC-94 was involved in a minor accident, as noted by the bent prop tip on #4.

In the Thule twilight a KC-97 approaches the field after another mission. (Lewis)

A B-47 comes home to McConnell AFB as the sun sets on the Kansas countryside. (Titus)

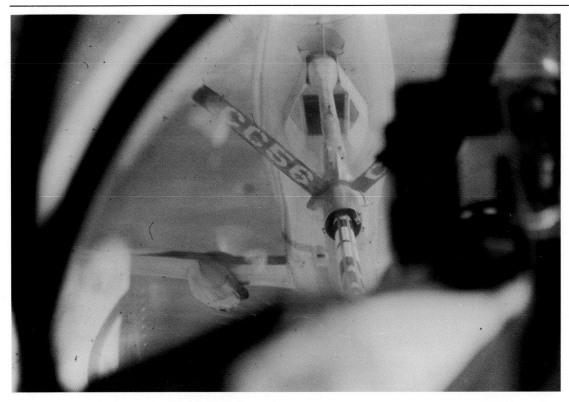

The tanker as viewed from the front seat of a B-47 during a routine airial refueling.(Titus)

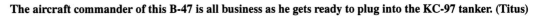

The aircraft commander of this B-47 is all business as he gets ready to plug into the KC-97 tanker. (Titus)

The ground crew of 310th BW B-47 #6228 makes final checks before the next mission during the 1959 Bomb Comp held at McCoy AFB, Florida. (USAF)

A B-47 taxies out for another training mission during 1956. (Titus)

B-47 (52-0554) awaits her crew so that another routine mission can get underway. (Titus)

A B-47 from the 40th BW at Smoky Hill AFB, Kansas over the Atlantic headed for England during a "Reflex" deployment.(Johnson)

B-47's on the flightline at McCoy AFB Florida, during the 1959 Bombing Competition. The 307th BW from Lincoln AFB Nebraska would win the meet and the Fairchild Trophy.(USAF)

A B-36J from the 92nd Bomb Wing. By the time of this 1956 airshow the 92nd was preparing to convert to the B-52. (Moffitt)

By the end of the 1950's, the KC-135 was being delivered to more units replacing the KC-97 as SAC's primary tanker. (Felling)

A most interesting photo of a B-52D (56-0688) dropping a string of bombs over what appears to be a snow covered landscape.(Campbell Archives)

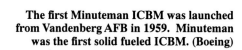

The first Minuteman ICBM was launched from Vandenberg AFB in 1959. Minuteman was the first solid fueled ICBM. (Boeing)

B-50D from the 96th Bomb Squadron, 2nd Bomb Wing at Hunter AFB, Georgia in 1951. (Harris)

KC-135 "City of Rome" was the first jet tanker to arrive at Griffis AFB, NY. (Moffitt)

Night Vigil-B52D (55-0112) from the 92nd BW at Fairchild AFB, Washington. Circa 1959.(Joe Bruch Collection)

RB-47E from the 90th Strat Recon Wing at Forbes AFB Kansas 1957. (Titus)

A B-47E at McConnell AFB waits for a paint job to restore the U.S. Air Force to her sides, 1956. (Titus)

Ground alert at SAC bases within the US and several overseas bases began on October 1, 1957. Aircraft were armed with nuclear weapons and ready to fly on a moments notice. (Johnson)

Right: The test program for the AGM-28 Hound Dog was conducted during the late 1950's. The SAC B-52G carries two test missles during a captive flight test. (Felling)

Below: An Oregon ANG F- 94 intercepts a B-36 during a training mission. Such intercepts were used to sharpen the defenses of both aircraft.(Toynbee)

RB-47E (51-22787) on the flightline McConnell AFB, Kansas, September 1959. (Author's Collection)

B-47E (51-2339) on the flightline McConnell AFB, Kansas, September 1959. (Author's Collection)

B-47E (53-2314) of the 509th BW carries the full white anti-nuclear flash belly paint in this May 1959 photo at Pease AFB, NH.(Burridge)

B-47E (52-0347) of the 98th BW on the flightline at Lincoln AFB Nebraska, July 1959. (Hill)

B-47's in one of the hangers at Tinker AFB during Project Milk Bottle May 23, 1958. (Tinker AFB Archives)

Project Milk Bottle envolved replacing the main wing attachment pins in the B-47 fleet. Outer wing panels were also replaced. (Tinker AFB Archives).

Above: A B-47 from the 68th BW about ready to clear the hanger after going through the Milk Bottle program at Tinker AFB, Oklahoma. (Tinker AFB Archives)

Left: Crewmen from the 44th BW prepare to accept a B-47 from Tinker AFB after it has gone through the Milk Bottle update. (Tinker AFB Archives)

From May to September 1958, Tinker AFB, Oklahoma processed 386 B-47's through the Milk Bottle program. (Tinker AFB Archives)

B-47's like these at Chelveston RAF, England stood ground alert during the three week "Reflex" period. (Moffitt)

In October 1957, SAC began phasing the B-47 out of service. The first to retire were the RB-47E's. Sitting on the ramp at Forbes AFB, 52-0749's days of service are numbered in this winter 1957 photo. (Titus)

The 95th BW at Biggs AFB, Texas was the last B-36 unit in SAC. This example from the 95th was photographed at Pease AFB in May 1958. (Burridge)

By February 1959, SAC's proud fleet of B-36's were all retired to the boneyard. (USAF)

Above: A C-45H from the 817th Air Base Group, Pease AFB ND, September 1957. (Burridge)

Above: SAC used the C-47 from 1946 till its retirement in 1971. This aircraft was photographed at Pease AFB in May 1958. (Burridge)

High over Kansas, a RB-47E from the 90th Strat Recon Wing refuels from a KC-97, in 1957. (Titus)

Tech orders 1019 and 1020 required an average of 2156 man hours to complete. (Tinker AFB Archives)

The last two KB-29P's (44-83956, 44-84075) assigned to the 27th ARS were retired from active service on November 25,1957.(Joe Bruch Collection)

By late 1958, ninety day rotation of entire wings were being replaced by three week "Reflex" of selected aircraft and crews to bases overseas. (Moffitt)

TB-25N (44-31464) of the 817th Air Base Group, Pease AFB, ND, May 1958. SAC used these aircrafts as utility aircraft. (Burridge)

A rare bird indeed was this C-123J assigned to Dow AFB, Maine in August 1959. The aircraft had a red tail and day-glo strip on tail fin and nose. Also noteworthy are the arctic skids. (Burridge)

F-84F's formed escort wings to guard SAC bombers on their way to targets.

SAC operated three squadrons of C-124's (50 aircraft) for about 10 years. SAC's airline carried every conceivable item possible, from spare parts, personnel, to cars and trucks. (Burridge)

In August 1960, Senator John F. Kennedy is briefed by a SAC crew on the airborne alert program. (Evely)

3
1960s

SAC moved deeper into the missile age by activating three Titan 1 squadrons and three Atlas E squadrons. To enhance these ICBM units, the first Snarks were placed on ground alert at Presque Island, Maine.

In August 1960, the first B-58 Hustler was accepted by the 43rd Bomb Wing at Carswell AFB, Texas. The B-58 was the first bomber capable of flying at supersonic speed, and to the crews, the new aircraft was certainly the hot rod of the bomber fleet.

As part of the ever growing alert posture, SAC completed "Project Open Road." The outcome of the project was the final form of the Minimum Interval Take Off. With the approval of the project, MITOs became a standard practice at SAC bases across the country. It was thrilling to watch all of the bobbing and weaving in the jetstream as the aircraft practice this breathtaking practice.

Along with "Open Road", SAC reached the goal of having at least one third of the bomber and tanker force on fifteen minute ground alert at all times. SAC's mailed fist was as ready as ever.

SAC B-58 Hustler crews started 1961 off with a BOOM! On January 12th a B-58 from the 43rd Bomb Wing set three world speed records. Just two days later these records were shattered by another B-58 and crew from the 43rd. With all the records being broken, the desert around Edwards AFB, reverberated with sonic booms.

On May 10th a B-58 from the 43rd won the Bleriot Cup for a sustained flight of 669.4 miles in thirty minutes, forty-five seconds at a speed of 1,302 miles per hour. The new bomber would continue to break and reset world records for its class for years to come. The Hustler held so many records that it could be said that it was in a class all by itself.

While the speedy Hustler was setting records, SAC took delivery of the first B-52H at Wurthsmith AFB, Michigan. The Hustler may have had the spotlight at the moment, but longevity would be the fame of the new "Cadillac" of the B-52 fleet.

The first Minuteman ICBM missile wing was activated in July. The 341st Strategic Missile Wing would call Malstrom AFB, Montana home. The new solid fuel missiles were buried in underground silos across the Montana countryside in the Great Falls area.

1962 was fairly quiet until October when SAC U-2s brought back photographic evidence of offensive missiles installations on the island of Cuba. On October 22nd, President John F. Kennedy

SAC has always referred to the B-52 as their "Big Stick." This 99th Bomb Wing B-52 (54-2673) was nicknamed THE BIG STICK. (Burridge)

January 12, 1960, MOHAWK VALLEY, a B-52G (58-0225) arrived at Griffis AFB, New York. This was the first B-52G to be assigned to the 4039th Strategic Wing. (Moffitt)

announced to a stunned nation that the United States would impose a quarantine against Cuba and demand the removal of the Soviet missiles. With that announcement, SAC went into high gear. The B-47 fleet was flushed from their bases and fanned out across the globe to their forward bases. The B-52s stepped up the airborne alert status. The missile wings were brought up to a moment's notice alert posture. For the next few days the world stood at the brink of nuclear confrontation.

The Soviet Union stepped back from the brink on October 28th when they agreed to remove the missiles from Cuba. Later they also agreed to remove medium bombers that had been stationed there, and the Cuban Missile Crisis wound down by late November. Later it was found that over ninety per cent of SAC's 1,600 bombers had been on fifteen minute alert during the crisis.

The so called "Missiles of October" had overshadowed the delivery of the last B-52H to Minot AFB and the last B-58 Hustler to Bunker Hill AFB. Both of the deliveries took place on October 26th.

A B-58 Hustler from the 305th Bomb Wing at Bunker Hill AFB, Indiana set a new speed record during Operation "Greased Lightning." The Hustler made the dash from Tokyo to London in eight hours, thirty five minutes at a sustained speed of 938 miles per hour on October 16, 1963.

The assassination of President Kennedy in November overshadowed the years' events. As usual in a time of national crisis, the Strategic Air Command increased its alert posture in the event a potential aggressor thought they could catch us napping during a period of national mourning.

1964 saw the decline of Reflex Operations to overseas bases by the B-47 fleet. As part of economic moves the aging B-47 fleet was being retired from active service. Along with the B-47s the prop driven KC-97s were also being phased out of active service.

On June 9th, SAC KC-135s refueled eight F-100s from the Tactical Air Command. This air refueling was special because the fighters were on their way to bomb Communist Pathet Lao emplacements in Laos. This marked the first combat support mission in Southeast Asia.

January of 1965 saw the activation of the 4252nd Strategic Wing at Kadena AFB, Okinawa to provide tanker support for current and future fighter operation in Southeast Asia.

On June 18th, twenty seven B-52s staged out of Anderson AFB, Guam and flew towards South Viet Nam. They dropped their loads on suspected Viet Cong targets and returned to Guam. The B-52 had dropped its first bombs in anger. The B-52s continued these long missions to Viet Nam through December.

With the B-52s flying "Arc Light" missions from Guam and the fighters flying daily support missions in Viet Nam, tankers from the Strategic Air Command flew over 4,000 support sorties during the last six months of the year.

Combat operations continued during 1966. B-52 sorties were designed to disrupt Viet Cong buildups and cut supply lines along

Assigned to the 43rd Bomb Wing this B-58 Hustler was used in Project White Horse. She spent the month of January at Ellsworth AFB, South Dakota testing how the B-58 would react to cold weather. (Joe Bruch Collection)

the Ho Chi Minh Trail. Over 5,000 B-52 sorties were flown during the year. Along with the B-52 missions the tanker crews were putting in a lot of overtime keeping the bombers and fighters loaded with fuel to complete the missions assigned to them.

While the B-52s were busy in Southeast Asia, SAC was busy retiring the last of the B-47 force. The last two active B-47 bombers left their respective bases on February 11th for the storage facility at Davis Monthan AFB.

SAC made the international news when a KC-135 (61-0273) and a B-52G (58-0256) crashed due to a mid-air collision during air refueling operations off the coast of Spain near Palomores on January 17th. The B-52 carried several nuclear weapons. Two weapons underwent non-nuclear detonation on impact with the ground. The United States paid for the clean up of contaminated soil. Another weapon was located off the shore and recovered by the Navy on April 17th.

During 1967, SAC B-52s flew over 9,000 sorties against targets in Southeast Asia. This was nearly double from the previous

year. On May 6th, the bomber force flew the 10,000 sortie since starting operations in Viet Nam.

Along with the bomber operations, the tankers were just as busy. During the year SAC tankers flew over 22,000 sorties and delivered over 1.1 million pounds of fuel in support of air operations in Southeast Asia.

Air operations continued during 1968. The defense of the outpost at Khe Sanh was the largest use of air power in a single area to date. Strategic Air Command B-52s pounded suspected areas of troop concentration and gun emplacements around the Marine base. During the siege of Khe Sanh, B-52s dropped over 60,000 pounds of bombs on suspected targets.

The Strategic Air Command finished the decade with continued air operations in Southeast Asia. In January the forward base at U-Tapao Thailand was converted to a primary B-52 base of operations. SAC tanker missions decreased slightly during the year. In spite of this decrease, it was safe to say that the tankers were still busy lowering the boom.

On July 1, 1960 an RB-47H (53-4281), similar to these RB-47Es, was shot down by Soviet aircraft over the Arctic near Norway. Only two members of the 55th Strategic Recon Wing crew survived. (Knapp)

T-33 (48-0676) complete with command sash. Note the U-2 on the tip tank which gives rise to the belief that this example served as a proficiency trainer with recon unit using the U-2 during the 1960s. (Esposito)

It seemed that every SAC base had several T-33s. They were used for a variety of roles. This example sports the SAC Command sash at mid fuselage. Photographed at Pease AFB, October 1960. (Burridge)

Known as the "Blue Canoe", the military version of the Cessna 210 was used for proficiency training and as a liaison aircraft. (Esposito)

B-47E (51-2433) sitting on the flightline at McConnell AFB, Kansas, September 24, 1960. (Author's Collection)

A B-52G with a load of experimental Hound Dog missiles on the ramp at McConnell AFB, Kansas, September 24, 1960. (Author's Collection)

Flushed from the molehole by the dreaded Klaxon, an alert crew from the 43rd Bomb Wing race towards their alert cocked B-58. (USAF)

KC-135A (59-1498) of the 100th Air Refueling Squadron is inspected by the open house crowd at Pease AFB, 1960. (Burridge)

The climax of Operation Blue Nose was the launch of a Hound Dog by a B-52G after a twenty hour captive flight to the North Pole and back on April 12, 1960. The test was listed as successful. (Fraser)

A B-52G from Seymour Johnson AFB prepares to take off during low level training missions code named "Oil Burner." (Ethell)

A B-52G with a brace of GAM-77 Hound Dog missiles during the final test phase at Edwards AFB, California. (USAF)

In the early 1960s, SAC was proud of showing off its two big sticks as this publicity photos shows a B-52 flying over an Atlas launch site at Vandenberg AFB, California. (SAC/PAO)

Another publicity photo showing a B-52G over a Titan I missile site during the early 1960s. (Joe Bruch Collection)

Under a NATO agreement the SM-78 (later PGM-19) Jupiter missile was deployed to forward bases in Italy and Turkey. This Jupiter was stationed near Gioia del Colle, Italy on May 16, 1960. (Joe Bruch Collection)

The Jupiter sites destined for Turkey never reached operational status. These missiles at Gioia del Colle were on alert status on July 14, 1960. (Joe Bruch Collection)

On July 1, 1960 SAC began testing the Airborne Command Post by placing a modified KC-135 on fifteen minute ground alert. As with all ground alert aircraft, the ability to refuel in the air was essential. (Starke)

This KC-135 slid off the runway at Offutt on January 2, 1961. Another few feet and she would have ended up on Highway 75, which runs just off the main runway. (Author's Collection)

B-58 (55-0672) was the second Hustler to be modified to TB-58 configuration. She served with the 43rd Bomb Wing. (GD)

B-58 (60-114) spent most of her service life with the 305th Bomb Wing at Bunker Hill AFB, Indiana. (Author's Collection)

A record setting Hustler and crew. Lt. Col. Howard Confer and his crew set three world records on January 14, 1961 while flying a B-58 Hustler from the 43rd Bomb Wing. (USAF)

B-58 Hustler (61-2051) was delivered to the 305th Bomb Wing at Bunker Hill AFB on December 1, 1961. (Joe Bruch Collection)

KC-97G (52-2708) from the 509th Bomb Wing opens her doors to the public during open house at Pease AFB, in October 1960. (Burridge)

B-58 Hustler (55-0670) after her conversion to a TB-58. She was delivered to the 43rd Bomb Wing on August 13, 1960. (Joe Bruch Collection)

A B-52G and crew from the 5th Bomb Wing take a short rest before the airshow crowd arrives at Pease AFB in October 1960. (Burridge)

This B-47E (53-4231) carries the shield of the 100th Bomb Wing. During World War II the 100th was called the "Bloody Hundredth" due to the high loss rate in combat. (Burridge

An H-43B from Base Rescue Flight, Pease AFB, May 1961. (Burridge)

An H-19 helicopter from Pease AFB, Rescue Flight, October 1960. (Burridge)

Taxing a fully loaded tanker can be dangerous. The right main gear folded, leaving 57-1509 in this predicament. (Author's Collection)

SAC's three Strategic Support Wings were phased out by the end of 1960. Their C-124s were retired or turned over to Military air Transport Service. (Joe Bruch Collection)

B-58 (60-1124) from the 305th Bomb Wing takes off from Bunker Hill AFB for a training mission. (Joe Bruch Collection)

The two B-58 wings operated several C-123s for support of the problem prone Hustler. (Esposito)

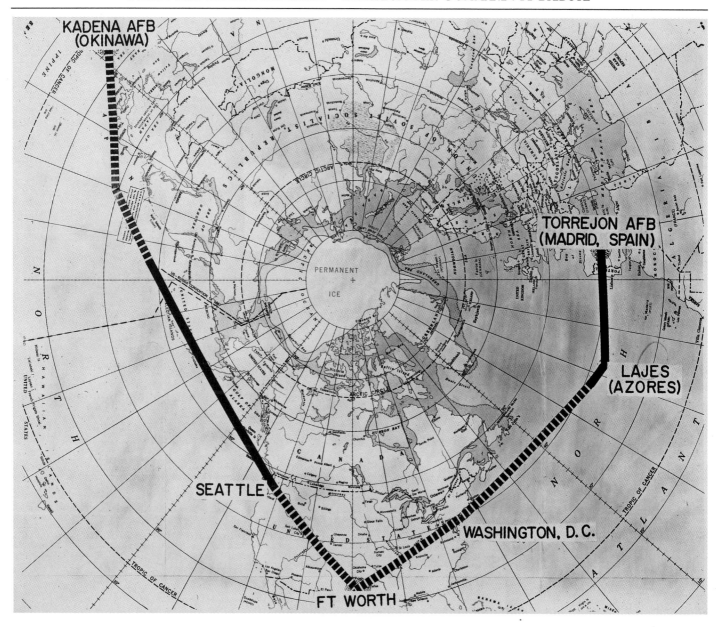

Above: Operation Persian Rug, January 10-11, 1962. The route covered 12,532.28 miles. This set a new non-stop non-refueled record that stood until "Voyager" flew around the world. The B-52 weighed in at 244 tons at take off. (Evely)

Opposite above: Typical Minot weather in January 1962. The crew of the B-52H (60-0040) prepare to leave the minus 35 degrees below zero and head for sunny Kadena AFB, Okinawa for the start of Operation Persian Rug. (Evely)

Opposite below: Major Clyde Evely and the Persian Rug crew after the record breaking flight at Torrejon AFB, Spain. Each of the crew was awarded the Distinguished Flying Cross. (Evely)

MISS MINOT, KC-135 (58-0098). She was the first tanker to arrive at Minot AFB, North Dakota and was assigned to the 4136th Strategic Wing in July 1961. (Joe Bruch Collection)

PEACE PERSUADER was the first B-52H (60-0025) to be delivered to the 4136 Strategic Wing at Minot AFB. (Tyree)

THE COWTOWN HUSTLER (59-2458) and the crew of Operation Heat Rise, March 5, 1962. (USAF)

The next to the last Hustler on the production line. She was delivered to the 305th Bomb Wing on October 26, 1962. She retired from active service December 19, 1969. (Joe Bruch Collection)

B-58 Hustler (58-1013) served with the 43rd Bomb Wing until she was retired. (Author's Collection)

The SM-62 Snark was declared operational on March 18, 1961 with the 702nd Strategic Missile Wing at Presque Island, Maine. On June 25, 1961 the Snark force was deactivated. (Joe Bruch Collection)

A night launch is always impressive, like this Snark launch from Coco Beach, Florida. (Joe Bruch Collection)

An Atlas D is loaded with propellants during a test exercise in June 1961. (GD)

The minuteman missile encased within this erector transporter will be lowered into the silo where it will stand alert and ready against attack. (Author's Collection)

A minuteman launch control complex under construction. The actual control area is housed within the dome shaped area. The chimney-like structure is the elevator. (Author's Collection)

Minuteman missile sites like this one are spread across the Dakotas, Montana, Wyoming, and Missouri. (Author's Collection)

Aerial view of a Minuteman launch control complex. The capsule with the two SAC launch control officers lies some fifty feet below. This complex controls ten missiles in the surrounding countryside. (Author's Collection)

The GAM-72 (later ADM-20) Quail was designed as a decoy missile. They were carried by B-52s and launched to confuse enemy radar. (Author's Collection)

A Quail decoy missile undergoing system checks in its handling cradle. The Quail served in SAC from 1960 to 1978. (Author's Collection)

The first launch of a Titan II conducted by a SAC missile crew occurred on September 23, 1963. (USAF)

The Titan I Missile became operational with the 703rd Strategic Missile Wing at Lowery AFB, Colorado on April 20, 1963. (Joe Bruch Collection)

B-52D (55-0100) drops a load of bombs on Viet Cong targets during a mission to the heartland of Vietnam. (Ethell)

Right: B-52F (57-0162) unloads on suspected Viet Cong targets in Vietnam, July 1965. (Ethell)

The Atlas missile had a short career with SAC. The last "E" version was removed from alert status at Lincoln AFB, Nebraska in April 1965. (Joe Bruch Collection)

The first Minuteman "ripple" launch was conducted by the 10th Strategic Missile Squadron from Malstrom AFB, Montana. The actual launch was conducted at Vandenberg AFB, California on February 29, 1964. (Felling)

An F-100 Super Sabre (55-3367) formates off the tankers wing after taking on a load of fuel in October 1961. (Moffitt)

In October 1965 Project Fly Fast directed that the last five B-47 Wings be phased out by June 1966. The mainstay of SAC's bomber force for many years would soon be a lonely figure in the sky. (Moffitt)

A SAC U-2 piloted by Major Richard Heyser brought back photographic evidence on the island of Cuba, October 1962. (Fraser)

Imagine going from a high performance jet bomber to trying for some flight time in a Blue Canoe. (Author's Collection)

In November 1961, SAC was assigned sole management of all KC-135 tankers. Air refueling by SAC tankers would include fighters as well as bombers. (Moffitt)

Above: Project FLY FAST phased out the B-47 from SAC's inventory. This B-47E (52-3363) left McConnell AFB, Kansas on July 17, 1964 and was photographed on her final flight to the storage facility at Davis Monthan AFB, Arizona. (Boeing)

A B-47E over the Atlantic headed for reflex duty in Spain during the summer of 1963. (Moffitt)

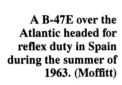

KC-135 (59-1512) was one of 54 tankers to be modified to refuel the SR-71 Blackbird. These aircraft were assigned to the 9th Strategic Recon Wing at Beale AFB, California. (Felling)

The 55th Strategic Recon Wing at Offutt AFB, Nebraska began continuous airborne command post operations on February 3, 1961, code name "Looking Glass." These aircraft flew in shifts that allowed one to be in the air at all times. (Boeing)

A B-58 Hustler plugs into the boom of a KC-135 during a November 1963 training mission. (Moffitt)

Fuel transfer complete, the Hustler begins to pull away. This refueling was accomplished with the Hustler flying on three engines. Note the afterburn lid position on the left inboard engine. The open position indicates the engine is either shut down or at idle. (Moffitt)

The Hustler drops below the tanker to continue the mission. (Moffitt)

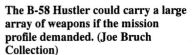

Operation Heat Rise, March 5, 1962. A B-58 Hustler from the 43rd Bomb Wing flew from Los Angeles to New York and back to Los Angeles, breaking three speed records. (Moffitt)

The Hustler made the round trip from Los Angeles to New York and back in 4 hours 41 minutes, 14.98 seconds. The average speed was 1,044.56 miles per hour down to refuel. (Moffitt)

The B-58 Hustler could carry a large array of weapons if the mission profile demanded. (Joe Bruch Collection)

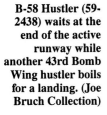

B-58 Hustler (59-2438) waits at the end of the active runway while another 43rd Bomb Wing hustler boils for a landing. (Joe Bruch Collection)

During the Missile Crisis SAC bombers and tankers flew countless hours of actual airborne nuclear alert. It was this posture of strength that the United States military projected that led to the Soviets backing down. (Moffitt)

Airborne alert missions were hard on aircraft and crews. This view from a B-52G on alert shows what the tanker looked like as the bomber approached the pre-contact stable position. (Moffitt)

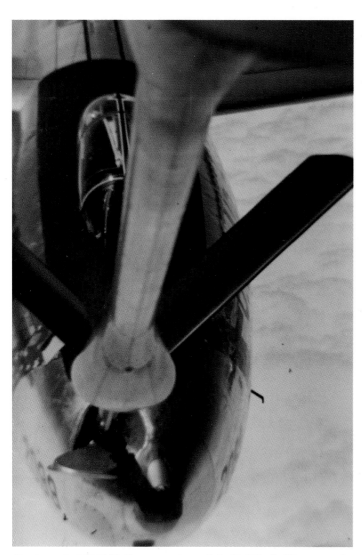

By the end of 1964, Reflex operations of the B-47 had all but ceased. This B-47 headed toward Torrejon AFB; Spain would become a thing of the past. (Moffitt)

On January 18, 1961 SAC announced to the public that combat armed B-52s were flying "airborne alert." These missions could last up to twenty-four hours. Aerial refueling kept these cocked bombers in the air. (Moffitt)

On June 9, 1964 SAC flew the first combat support sorties. Code named YANKEE TEAM TANKER FORCE they refueled eight F-100 fighters bound for an air strike against anti-aircraft emplacements on the Plain of Jars, Laos. (Moffitt)

Looking out the windshield of a KC-135 during the beginning of a three tanker Minimum Interval Take Off (MITO). (Moffitt)

Rolling down the runway at Griffis AFB just 15 seconds behind the lead tanker. (Moffitt)

Lots of JP-4 smoke traces the tankers path as the MITO gets airborne during the three ship cell. (Moffitt)

This early 1960s view of the underground Command Post shows that the 307th Bomb Wing at Lincoln, Nebraska is in the middle of a dreaded no notice Organizational Readiness Inspection. (Joe Bruch Collection)

Current operations are projected onto the big wall screens. The information is used by the battle staff to make decisions affecting SAC bases around the world. (Joe Bruch Collection)

Three stories below the plains of Nebraska men of the headquarters staff maintain their vigil in the famed underground command post. (Joe Bruch Collection)

This 380th Bomb Wing B-47E rolls out with approach and drag chutes flopping in the slipstream during Reflex deployment to Chelveston, England in July 1963. (Moffitt)

B-52G (58-0248) on the Tinker AFB flightline showing the repair kits and support vehicles needed to keep the aircraft flying. (Tinker AFB Archives)

B-47E (53-1955) from the 380th Bomb Wing at Plattsburg AFB, New York, June 12, 1965. (Mayer)

B-52Fs from the 2nd Bomb Wing at Barksdale AFB prepare to launch during a no notice alert in 1964. (Joe Bruch Collection)

An early KC-135 on the flightline at Griffis AFB, New York in 1962. (Moffitt)

This KC-135 was the first tanker with the modified tall tail and power assisted rudder to be delivered to Griffis AFB, New York in 1964. (Moffitt)

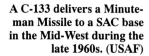

A C-133 delivers a Minuteman Missile to a SAC base in the Mid-West during the late 1960s. (USAF)

Off-loading the Minuteman from the cargo plane was a tricky undertaking. Clearance was minimum, requiring great care. (USAF)

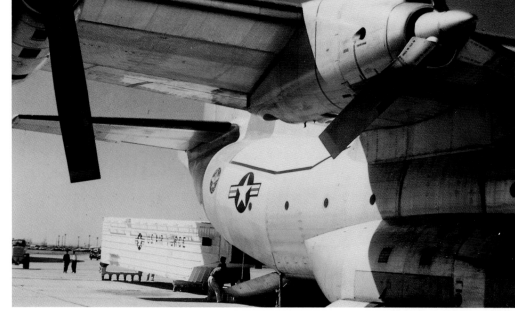

B-58 (59-2457) from the 43rd Bomb Wing on the ramp at Carswell AFB, Texas. (Fraser)

Disaster struck Alaska on March 27, 1967 in the form of an earthquake. The next morning two B-58s from the 43rd Bomb Wing flew over the devastation taking photographs from 500 feet. The photos were delivered to SAC Headquarters fourteen hours, thirty-eight minutes after SAC was handed the mission. (Fraser)

Even sitting on the ground, the Hustler appeared to be doing Mach 2. (Fraser)

The B-58 Hustler's first Bomb Comp was in 1960, five months after the 43rd Bomb Wing received the first Hustler. During the competition a 43rd Bomb Wing Hustler set a record by getting underway two minutes and ten seconds after the Klaxon sounded. (USAF)

B-58A (61-2074) of the 305th BW at McDill AFB for open house in May 1969. (Moffitt)

SAC flew the 10,000th B-52 sortie on May 6, 1967. The last B-52D BIG BELLY modified B-52D was delivered in October. SAC's big stick continued to soldier on. (Forsberg)

In 1968 four SR-71 Blackbirds were deployed to Kadena AFB to conduct recon operations in Southeast Asia. SR-71A (64-17974) was one of the four aircraft. (Author's Collection)

A crew chief directs his B-52 out of the hardstand for another mission. (Ethell)

The third FB-111 (67-7195) was delivered to the 340th Bomb Wing at Carswell AFB in December 1969. (USAF)

B-52G (59-2590) at a McDill AFB, Florida airshow May 1969. (Moffitt)

RC-135U (64-14849) from the 55th Strategic Recon Wing. (Author's Collection)

The long flight "across the pond" is over. The tired crew will debrief on how the flight went. The ground crews will start working to get the aircraft "cocked" for ground alert. (Moffitt)

UH-19 Chikasaw helicopter on the flight line at Little Rock AFB, Arkansas June 29, 1967. SAC used the UH-19 as a rescue, utility, and missile site transport aircraft. (Burridge)

A B-52D leaves Anderson AFB, Guam for a ARC LIGHT mission to Vietnam in 1968. (USAF)

MEKONG EXPRESS (57-0144) on March 21, 1966 with eighty missions to her credit while assigned to the 320th Bomb Wing (Prov) at Anderson AFB, Guam. (Author's Collection)

ERB-47H (53-6240) from the 55th Strategic Recon Wing on the ramp at Tan Son Nhut AFB, Republic of Viet Nam, April 13, 1966 after a Viet Cong mortar attack. (USAF)

A nuclear armed B-52G lifts from the runway at Griffis AFB to go on station for airborne alert in April 1962. (Moffitt)

Dense clouds of black smoke follow this KC-135 into the air at Griffis AFB, New York. Even with water injection the tanker uses ninety percent of the runway in a max weight take off. (Moffitt)

Heading West into the sunset during an ARC LIGHT mission during 1968. Missions from Anderson AFB, Guam averaged twelve hours. (Harris)

Contrails streaming back in the cold air at 38,000 feet. The view behind the co-pilot of a B-47 was spectacular. (Johnson)

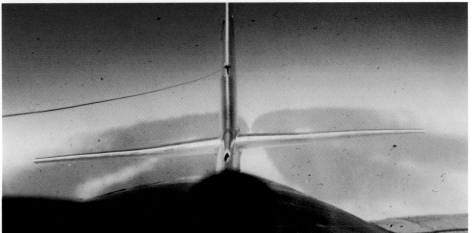

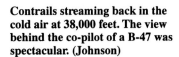

Viewed from the ground a MITO was always loud and exciting. The MITO was developed to launch as many alert aircraft as possible in the event of an attack. (Moffitt)

Buff Sunrise at Anderson AFB, Guam 1968. (USAF)

Secretary of Defense Robert McNamara announced that SAC would obtain an updated version of the F-111A fighter. Designated the FB-111 it would replace the B-58 and older B-52s that were being phased out. (Fraser)

The sixth production SR-71 Blackbird on a flight near Edwards AFB. SAC crews flew this aircraft for test and evaluation. (AFFTC/HO)

By the last part of 1969 the B-58 Hustler was being phased out of SAC's inventory. B-58 (59-2456) is shown carrying four Mark 43 practice weapons on external stores racks. She was retired on December 9, 1969. (Joe Bruch Collection)

TB-58 (55-0671) from the 43rd Bomb Wing banks away from the tanker during a training mission. Note that this aircraft is carrying only the top half of the two component pod. (Knapp)

During the Cuban Missile Crisis in 1962, SAC dispersed the B-47 fleet to all corners of the world so they would be closer to their potential targets. (Joe Bruch Collection)

B-52H (60-0034) taxies out to take off and go on station for airborne alert during the Cuban Missile Crisis. (Joe Bruch Collection)

B-52Gs of the 4039th Strategic Wing on the ramp at Griffis AFB, New York. On February 1, 1963 the 4039th was inactivated and replaced by the 416th Bomb Wing. (Moffitt)

A 96th Bomb Wing B-47 comes home to roost at Dyess AFB, Texas. (Harris)

The low level flights were aptly named as the B-52s used a lot of fuel and produced dark clouds of smoke. This B-52G is landing at Seymour Johnson AFB after an Oil Burner mission on February 2, 1960. (Ethell)

This B-52D (56-0601) attempted a landing at Da Nang after the loss of electrical power and other systems. It used over 5,000 feet of runway before touching down. She went off the end of the runway and exploded. Only the tail gunner survived this July 8, 1967 accident. (Joe Bruch Collection)

Nosewheel problems caused this KC-135 (58-0018) to end up covered with foam after the accident. She was repaired and is still flying. (Author's Collection)

Ground refueling could be dangerous. KC-135 (56-3657) is completely enveloped in flames in the 1962 photo taken at Attus AFB, Oklahoma. (Tinker AFB Archives)

SAC bases never closed due to the weather. A snow plow clears the white stuff from the flightline at Minot AFB, North Dakota during the 1960s. (5th BW)

Security Police maintain a silent vigil in the blowing snow. The B-52H is standing ground alert at Minot AFB, North Dakota. (5th BW)

Ground crews remove a NODAK snowfall in order to download a Hound Dog missile. (5th BW)

With the snow removed the crew can download the Hound Dog from this 450th Bomb Wing B-52 at Minot. (5th BW)

A C-123 Provider used by the 305th Bomb Wing in Support of the B-58 Hustler program. (Joe Bruch Collection)

Many times crews from SAC have been called upon to provide humanitarian services. This rescue of two boys from the Spokane River occurred on March 29, 1964. (Joe Bruch Collection)

A C-47 (44-8411) from the 817th Air Base Group, Pease AFB, New Hampshire. The old Gooney Bird was still going strong in this May 1968 photo. (Burridge)

This B-52H (60-0014) is from the 410th Bomb Wing at K.I. Sawyer AFB, Michigan. (Eisehart)

This B-52F (57-0164) from the 320th Bomb Wing flew over fifty-five missions from Anderson AFB, Guam during 1965-66. (Ethell)

Ground crewmen load the external racks of a B-52F with 750 pound bombs before a mission against suspected Viet Cong targets. (USAF)

B-52F (57-0153) of the 320th Bomb Wing leaves Anderson AFB, Guam on June 18, 1965 on the first B-52 mission of the Vietnam War. (USAF)

The first B-52 (52-8711) delivered to SAC now wears the unit crest of the 22nd Bomb Wing at March AFB, California. She was photographed during a practice alert in June 1965. (USAF)

This B-47E wears a well worn unit crest of the 98th Bomb Wing from Lincoln AFB, Nebraska. (Author's Collection)

She was known as LUCKY LADY III when she led Operation Power Flight in 1957. In May 1965 she wore CITY OF EL PASO on her sides.

B-52G (58-0179) photographed at the moment the right inboard engine pod erupts into fire during a missed approach to Seymore Johnson AFB on May 6, 1964. (Williams)

The flightline at Anderson AFB, Guam is full of B-52s during this 1964 deployment. (Ethell)

Missile technicians upload a Hound Dog missile to a B-52H at Seymour-Johnson AFB in June 1967. (Joe Bruch Collection)

A B-52D departs Anderson AFB, Guam for a mission in Vietnam. During the siege of the Marine base at Khe San, SAC B-52s dropped over 60,000 tons of bombs on enemy positions around the base. (USAF)

Hustler (61-2061) on the flight line at Bunker Hill AFB. This aircraft crashed near Darrazett, Texas in June 14, 1967. (Joe Bruch Collection)

B-52 Hustler (59-2436) from the 43rd Bomb Wing returns to the Carswell runway after a training mission. (GD)

CANNONBALL was actually B-58A (59-2434) from the 43rd Bomb Wing. She was retired on December 17, 1969. (Joe Bruch Collection)

Known as CITY OF KOKOMA, B-52 (60-1119) from the 305th Bomb Wing crashed near McKinney, Kentucky during a practice mission on December 12, 1966. (Joe Bruch Collection)

TB-58 (55-0672) photographed at Lincoln AFB in 1964. She was originally built as a YB-58 and was the 13th airframe built. (Hill)

In April 1965 a RB-47H like this one from the 55th Strategic Recon Wing was attacked by North Korea Migs while on patrol in international waters. After a furious engagement the MiGs were turned away. With two engines out and a third at partial power, the aircraft landed at Yakota AFB. The RB-47 was written off due to the damage. (Joe Bruch Collection)

The B-47 phase of Project Fly Fast was completed on February 11, 1966. A B-47E from Pease AFB and one from Mountain Home AFB were flown to the storage facility at Davis Monthan, AFB. (Joe Bruch Collection)

December 29, 1967 the last B-47 serving in SAC prepares to leave Offutt AFB, Nebraska. The RB-47H (53-4296) would be stored at Davis-Monthan AFB. (USAF)

The last B-47 built started her career with the 40th Bomb Wing at Schilling AFB, Kansas. She retired from active duty with the 307th Bomb Wing and was sent to the Air Force Museum at Dayton. (USAF)

Through the "Looking Glass." EC-135 (61-0287) refuels 61-0262. Both are Airborne Launch Control Center aircraft. (Starke)

A rare bird, this aircraft started as a KC-135A (59-1491). She was modified to an RC-135D then updated to RC-135S standards. She was operated by the 6th Strategic Recon Wing at Eilson AFB, Alaska until she crashed on March 10, 1969. (Joe Bruch Collection)

B-52D (56-0069) at U-Tapao AFB, Thailand. She was on a short deployment to Thailand because of Typhoon Olga. (USAF)

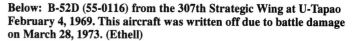

Below: B-52D (55-0116) from the 307th Strategic Wing at U-Tapao February 4, 1969. This aircraft was written off due to battle damage on March 28, 1973. (Ethell)

Above: Of the three nearest B-52s only 56-0689 will survive the Vietnam war. She is preserved at Duxford, UK. 55-0097 was salvaged after an inflight fire February 13, 1973. 55-0676 crashed on takeoff at U-Tapao July 19, 1969. (USAF)

B-52D (65-0678) lifts off the runway at U-Tapao for a mission in February 1969. (Ethell)

B-25D (56-0615) drops its load of bombs during stepped up operations against targets near Saigon in 1969. (USAF)

THE MEKONG EXPRESS (57-0144) unloads on a Viet Cong target during one of her eighty-six missions. (Harris)

B-52Ds drop their strings of 750 pound bombs on enemy targets during an ARC LIGHT mission in 1967. (Ethell)

A B-52G armed with a pair of Hound Dog missiles leaves the runway in a cloud of black smoke during a practice scramble. (Ethell)

4
1970s

W hen SAC entered the 1970s, the command listed 1,159 tactical aircraft. Along with these aircraft, SAC carried a ready force of 982 Minuteman and 57 Titan II ICBMs. To compliment this there were 345 Hound Dog stand-off missiles.

Bombing operations in Southeast Asia continued to dominate the flying schedule. There was a slight decrease in the actual number of combat missions flown by B-52s. However, the tankers kept up their record pace in support of the fighters.

The last two B-58 Hustlers were retired to Davis Monthan on January 16th. The speedy bombers had been slated to go to Southeast Asia but the project was canceled at the last moment. SAC's record-setting supersonic bomber had been in service for just over a decade.

June saw the first flight of ten Minuteman III ICBMS accepted by the 741st Strategic Missile Squadron at Minot AFB, North Dakota. These missiles carried the Mark 12 Multiple Independently Targetable Reentry Vehicle (MIRV) nuclear warheads.

June 1971 saw SAC start the seventh year of bombing operations in Southeast Asia. Missions were flown in support of ground forces, as well as to disrupt supply lines coming in from the north.

Combat operations dominated 1972. In April, Communist forces launched attacks at Quang Tri, Kontum and AnLoc. SAC countered with B-52 strikes to support ground operations and cut the enemy's supply lines. KC-135s continued to refuel tactical and

B-52F (57-0160) on a short final. SAC began retiring the B-52F fleet in September 1971. (Ethell)

strategic aircraft at a record pace. As operations continued the "tanker toads" racked up countless "saves."

In an effort to bring the North Vietnamese back to the Paris Peace Talks, President Nixon ordered the bombing of North Viet Nam to begin again. On December 18th the B-52s went "downtown" for the first mission of what would become known as "The Eleven Day War." Officially known as Operation Linebacker II, the bombing campaign would become the high and low point of SAC operations in Southeast Asia.

The first night of operations saw over two hundred SAMs (Surface To Air Missiles) fired at the attacking B-52s. Three B-52s were lost while three more were damaged. Of the 129 B-52s dispatched for the mission, 121 were listed as having an effective sortie.

Night two was a repeat of the first. B-52s went in from the same direction and altitude as the previous night. Post target turns were the same. To put it bluntly (as the SAC aircrews did) the SAC planners were asking for it. They got it on the third night.

There had been no change in tactics despite the pleas of the aircrews. The B-52s showed up at about the same time, altitude and from the same direction. The North Vietnamese were waiting. A total of six B-52s were shot down by SAMs. SAC flightcrews were next to mutiny over the fact that the mission planners had continued to use the same tactics for three night without a hint of change.

B-52s continued to go downtown on the fourth day of the bombing offensive. The number of BUFFs had been reduced and tactics had been changed. With the change in tactics and reduced sortie rate losses decreased.

A B-52D leaves Guam for the long flight to the target area during Linebacker II. (Ethell)

EC-135 (63-8053) crosses the fence at Offutt during a routine Looking Glass operation. (Hill)

By the last missions on December 29th, many of the SAC aircrews believed that if the missions continued, they could fly the missions during the day without the cover of darkness.

During Linebacker II operations, SAC B-52s had flown 724 sorties, and accounted for over 15,000 tons of bombs dropped on targets in and around Hanoi/Hiaphong. The defenses the aircrews encountered were the heaviest ever observed. The North Vietnamese fired over 1242 SAMs at the attacking B-52s. In all there were fifteen B-52s lost to SAMs. This amounted to an overall loss rate of 2.1 per cent. This was deemed more then acceptable in view of the fact that the SAM had been developed especially to combat American bombers like the B-52.

The Linebacker missions had accomplished exactly what had been intended. On December 30th, the North Vietnamese officials announced that they had a willingness to return to the peace table and begin a new round of "meaningful talks" towards a solution in Southeast Asia.

For the first two weeks of 1973, SAC bombers continued to bomb specified targets in North Viet Nam. On January 14th bombing operations came to a close in the North and on the 27th the Paris Peace Accords ended air operations over North Viet Nam, however, SAC B-52s did continue operations against communist positions in Laos and Cambodia.

In March 1972, the first AGM-69A Short Range Attack Missile (SRAM) was delivered to the 42nd Bomb Wing at Loring AFB, Maine. (USAF)

During the conventional operations in Viet Nam, SAC had always maintained its alert posture back home in the United States. B-52Hs had maintained the nuclear vigil while the missiles remained nestled in the silos acting as a deterrent to any brash moves by the Soviet Union. With peace in Viet Nam, SAC continued to maintain a powerful posture.

1975 saw the transfer of some tanker aircraft to the Reserve and Air National Guard. These units would be under the direct control of SAC in a time of national emergency. Although they were called week end warriors they still wore the SAC sash and worked under the standards of the command.

In November the 1st Airborne Command and Control Squadron was transferred to the control of SAC. The command now had the responsibility in getting the President off the ground in the event of a national crisis.

Flight testing for the new B-1 bomber continued in 1976, and things were looking very good for this new supersonic bomber. With the test program going smoothly the go ahead was given for full production. Along with the testing of the B-1, testing of the Air Launch Cruise Missile began in March. A successful test launch was conducted by a B-52G over the White Sands Range on the 5th. The ALCM was designed to increase the stand off capability of the B-52 and future B-1 fleets.

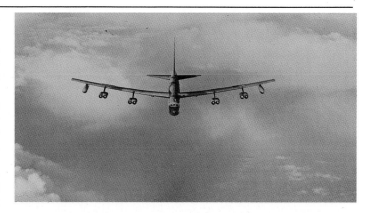

During 1970, B-52 ARC LIGHT missions declined from the previous years, but there was no sign of peace in Southeast Asia. (Ethell)

1977 was a year for cut backs and cancellations for new military programs. The power structure in Washington didn't seem to care or didn't realize that they were cutting the military back to dangerous levels of non-readiness. President Jimmy Carter announced on February 20th the cancellation of the already planned advanced cargo/tanker aircraft. In June, the White House announced that the B-1 had been canceled in favor of the Cruise Missile. The aging B-52 would be modernized and updated to fill the role of the manned bomber as it had for many years.

Changes and cutbacks continued into 1978. Older B-52 models were headed to the bone yard, and at the same time the Quail decoy missiles and the Hound Dog stand off missiles were marked for retirement as well.

As a mark of real change within the command, the first female flight officers began to pull ground alert duty at bases around the country. All female crew members were assigned to the tanker force thus assuring the policy of no females in combat. While women were pulling ground alert for the tankers, they were also starting to pull alert duty at the Titan II missile sites at McConnell AFB, Kansas.

SAC implemented the Single Integrated Operational Plan (SIOP) for the first time during Global Shield 1979. This exercise did everything short of actual nuclear warfare that would be done in the event of a nuclear confrontation. B-52s and tankers were alerted, with many flying to dispersal bases across the United States. On July 10th, as part of Global Shield, two Minuteman III missiles were launched from Vandenberg AFB, California. The exercise culminated with the launch of all aircraft that were standing ground alert. The countryside reverberated with the sound of jet engines. Clouds of dense black JP-4 smoke drifted across the countryside as the bomber and tankers were flushed from the alert pads.

B-52D (56-678) leaves U-Tapao with a full load headed for Hanoi. (Ethell)

A late afternoon launch of a Titan II from Vandenberg AFB, California. (Fraser)

The only surviving SR-71B #956 over the California countryside during a training sortie on July 23, 1971. (Harris)

SAC KC-135 tankers were credited with numerous "saves" when fighters were low on fuel. Here a bomb laden F-4E refuels on the way to a target. (Author's Collection)

Blackbird #975 takes on fuel at the rate of 5,500 pounds/minute. After about twelve minutes on the boom, she will be headed back to her high altitude cruise. (James)

SR-71B #956 pulls away from a tanker after topping off her fuel
tanks during a 1971 flight. (Harris)

The last two B-58 Hustlers from the 305th Bomb Wing officially retired from service on January 16, 1970. The
Hustler had served SAC for just ten years. (GD)

The business end of a Titan II receives special attention from technicians during an open silo systems check. (Joe Bruch Collection)

The 90th Strategic Missile Wing at Francis E. Warren AFB, Wyoming was the first unit to obtain combat readiness with the Minuteman III missile in 1973. (USAF)

Missile technicians run a series of checks on a Titan missile before placing it back on alert. (Fraser)

Bathed in fire, a minuteman is launch from Vandenburg. On December 13, 1971 the 91st Strategic Missile Wing at Minot accepted the last of the Minuteman III "G" series. This was the first unit to use the new multiple impact warheads (MIRV). (Boeing)

The SR-71B waits for a KC-135Q to clear the area before taking off on
another training mission. (Harris)

During the Vietnam war SR-71s staged from Kadena, Okinawa. Locals called them HABU because of their
resemblance to a snake that is native to the island. (USAF)

The 55th Strategic Recon Wing, LOOKING GLASS, flew the 100,000th accident-free mission on October 13, 1971. (Author's Collection)

On July 7, 1971, VC-47 (47-6326) became the last C-47 to retire from active duty in SAC. She last served with the 97th Bomb Wing at Blytheville AFB, Arkansas. The aircraft was placed on display at the U.S.S. Alabama Memorial Park at Mobile, Alabama. (Hill)

In spite of the losses during the previous night. The B-52s were readied for another mission. Here (55-0680) awaits her crew. (USAF)

B-52D (56-0690) safe at Tapao after her first Linebacker II mission.

B-52D (56-0677) headed out for another mission from U-Tapao. She survived her tour of duty in Southeast Asia only to crash near Wendover, Utah on July 30, 1972. (USAF)

The last B-52H built (61-0040) on a rain covered ramp in 1971. (Author's Collection)

B-52G (57-6488) wears the shield of the 28th Bomb Wing in this November 18, 1972 photo at March AFB, California. (LaBouy)

FB-111A (68-0292) at Naval Air Station, LeMoore, October 10, 1971. (LaBouy)

The B-52H fleet was constantly updated. Here 61-0040, the last B-52 built, undergoes modification and update at Tinker AFB, Oklahoma. (Author's Collection)

The flight crew climbs the steps to their SR-71 at Beale AFB, California for a mission on February 4, 1972. (Harris)

The crew chief directs the SR-71 from its "Blackbird Barn" on February 4, 1972. (Harris)

The Blackbird heads for the active runway under cloudy California skies. (Harris)

Blackbird in the barn. Groundcrew run #975 through a series of checks before the next mission. (USAF)

Blackbird #975 on the ramp at Beale AFB, California in February 1975. (Author's Collection)

Blackbirds were kept in the special bird houses when not flying. This protected them from the elements as well as prying eyes and satellites. (USAF)

Thousands of man hours went into loading the B-52s with bombs for the upcoming missions. (Ethell)

B-52s taxi out for the first Linebacker II mission on December 18, 1972. (Ethell)

The tail gunner's view of the wing lining up for a mission. (Carroll)

A belly full of bombs destined for a target in North Vietnam during Operation Linebacker II. (Nash)

B-52D (56-0693) ready for the mission on December 19, 1972.

B-52s on the flightline at Anderson AFB, Guam during December 1972. The nearest BUFF (56-0618) survived her missions. (Author's Collection)

While her sister BUFFs were fighting a hot war in Vietnam B-52H (60-0019) maintained alert against a possible Soviet attack on the United States. (Author's Collection)

Linebacker II showed that the B-52G was more susceptible to battle damage than her older sister. This B-52G is on the flightline at Anderson AFB, Guam, ready for a mission. (Ethell)

S/Sgt. Sam Turner was credited with the first B-52 Mig kill while flying as tail gunner on B-52D (56-0676) from the 307th Strategic Wing on December 18, 1972. (Joe Bruch Collection)

Between December 18-29, 1972, SAC tankers flew over 1300 sorties in support of Linebacker II operations. Aerial refueling was an around the clock operation. (USAF)

Another Mig 21 was shot down by these guns on December 24, 1972. Credit for the Mig went to Airman First Class Al Moore from the 307th Strategic Wing. That brought the score to Buffs two, Migs zip. (Carroll)

The night of December 20, 1972 was a disaster for the Linebacker crews. A total of six B-52s were shot down by North Vietnamese Surface to Air Missiles (SAMs). (Fraser)

The last B-52H built, on the ramp at Tinker AFB, Oklahoma. (Author's Collection)

During Linebacker II B-52s flew 724 sorties, dropping over 15,287 tons of bombs on fifty-nine targets. Fifteen BUFFs were lost to SAMs. This equated to a 2.1 percent loss rate for the force. (Fraser)

Operations at U-Tapao were hectic. Both tankers and bombers operated from the base during the Eleven Day air war. (Eisenhart)

Blackbird #972 lands in England after record setting a New York to London flight on September 1, 1974. The flight took one hour fifty-four minutes and fifty-six seconds for an average speed of 1,806.96 mph. (Joe Bruch Collection)

SR-71 (64-17972) at the Farnburough show after her record run from New York to London. (Author's Collection)

The crew of SR-71 (64-17963) prepare to light the fires for another mission. (Diveney)

At 26,000 feet a Blackbird gets a drink of JP-7 from a KC-135Q. The boom not only transfers fuel but acts as a secure intercom for transmitting messages from tanker to receiver. (James)

A KC-135 prepares to refuel an F-111 during a training mission somewhere over the western mountains. (USAF)

FB-111A (68-0288) from the 380th Bomb Wing on the transient ramp at Vance AFB, Oklahoma, April 12, 1974. (Rotramer)

FB-111A (67-7195) from the 509th Bomb Wing photographed at Whiteman AFB, Missouri on June 22, 1974. (Author's Collection)

FB-111A (68-026) at McConnell AFB, Kansas May 18, 1975. (USAF)

FB-111A (68-0257) at McConnell AFB, Kansas May 16, 1976. (USAF)

On January 2, 1975 an EC-135 Looking Glass like this one from the 55th Strategic Recon Wing recorded the 690th consecutive on-time take off for a mission. (Author's Collection)

Airborne battle staff on an EC-135 Looking Glass. They would be responsible for post nuclear attack command and control of any response by SAC. (Harris)

An EC-135 (61-0289) from the 4th Airborne Command and Control Squadron, 28th Bomb Wing on the alert ramp at Minot, September 2, 1975. (Miller)

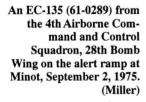

B-52H (60-0061) crosses the fence at McCoy AFB, Florida during the 1971 "Giant Voice" bombing competition. (Ethell)

B-52G CITY OF BOSSIER CITY from the 2nd Bomb Wing at Barksdale AFB was one of the representative aircraft in the 1974 Bombing/Navigation Competition. (Ethell)

On November 1, 1978 B-52D (56-0665) arrives at the Air Force Museum from the 97th Bomb Wing, Blytheville, Arkansas. A combat veteran, she was damaged by a SAM on April 9, 1972. (USAF)

An AGM-86B cruise missile falls from the pylon of a B-52G during a test. The first launch of a cruise missile was in March 1976. (Ethell)

The trademark of the J-57 engine was its ability to turn JP-4 into billowing clouds of black smoke. Here a B-52 uses water alcohol injection to get off the ground during a scramble alert. (Ethell)

Another BUFF lurks in the black smoke during a no notice launch exercise. (Ethell)

Cruising at 30,000 feet, EC-135 (63-8046) holds formation for this beautiful portrait. (Joe Bruch)

In April 1975 one hundred twenty-eight KC-135s were transferred to the Reserve and Air Guard. These tankers displayed the SAC shield and were under SAC's control in time of crisis. (Boeing)

KC-135 (59-1468) from the 100th Air Refueling Wing on the transient ramp at Andrews AFB, May 12, 1978. (Miller)

The Ohio Air National Guard's 160th Air Refueling Group was the first unit to receive the KC-135 on April 18, 1975. This KC-135 was photographed September 15, 1979. (Hare)

SAC acquired the 1st Airborne Command and Control Squadron on November 1, 1975. With the change, SAC added the E-4A to its inventory of aircraft. (Joe Bruch Collection)

President Jimmy Carter was the first president to fly on a E-4 NECAP aircraft on February 11, 1977. The aircraft pictured is the E-4B. (Joe Bruch Collection)

Casey 01 (57-2588) was the personal aircraft for the Commander of the Strategic Air Command. (Truax)

As part of the Bicentennial celebration, 64-17958 sits on the flightline at Andrews AFB on July 4, 1976. (Author's Collection)

Blackbird (64-17961) is pulled into position for the airshow at March AFB, California in October 1976. (Author's Collection)

SR-71 (64-17963) on the airshow line at Carswell AFB, Texas in October 1976. (Author's Collection)

Blackbird #972 landing at what is
believed to be Kadena AFB, Okinawa
in the 1970s. (Author's Collection)

SR-17 (64-17964) at Offutt
AFB, Nebraska for an
airshow in July 1979.
(Pickett)

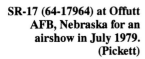

SR-71 (64-17972) over the runway at Mildenhall, RAF,
England May 1976. (USAF)

Blackbird (64-17964) at
Offutt AFB, July 1979.
(Pickett)

FB-111A (68-0279) from the 509th Bomb Wing at the Andrews AFB airshow May 1978. (Miller)

The second FB-111A (67-71940) taxies out of a Vark hut for a mission. FB-111A units would dominate the annual bombing competition, winning the Fairchild Trophy nine times in ten years. (GD)

FB-111A (68-0252) photographed July 16, 1978. (USAF)

FB-111A (68-0254) photographed in March 1977. (Author's Collection)

FB-111A (58-0247) of the 509th Bomb Wing begins a training sortie during the 1970s. (GD)

FB-111A (68-0270) at McGuire AFB, June 16, 1979. (GD)

The 509th Bomb Wing was one of two units to fly the FB-111A during its service with SAC. (GD)

Operations of the 100th Strategic Recon Wing were unknown during the Vietnam War. They flew the DC-130 armed with the Firebee drones. These "Buffalo Hunter" drones gathered photos and intelligence over North Vietnam. (Joe Bruch Collection)

The 9th Strategic Recon Wing was the only SAC wing to have T-38s assigned as SAC aircraft. Other units use the T-38 but they are actually Air Training Command aircraft. (Hill)

A two-tone grey U-2 on approach to an English base after a recon mission. (USAF)

U-2R (61-0340) at March AFB, California in October 1976. (Author's Collection)

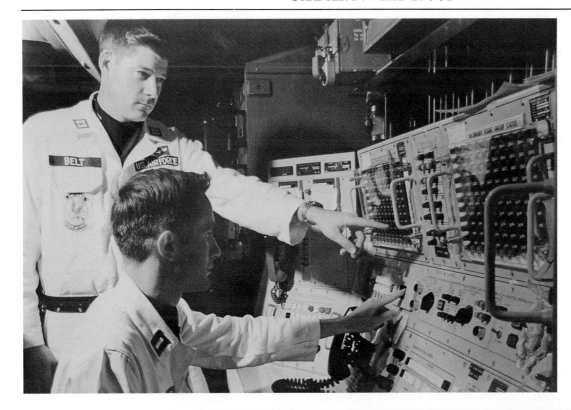

On alert missile crewmen go through systems checks in a Minuteman Launch Control Facility. (Fraser)

By the late 1970s, Minuteman sites dotted the countryside in the midwest and northern tier of the United States. (Boeing)

Acres of B-47s at Davis Monthan AFB in March 1971. Note that 52-0365 carries a TEE TOWN ECM pod on her side. (USAF)

Hustlers as far as the eye can see in this 1975 photo of the storage area at Davis Monthan AFB. (Author's Collection)

Once the pride of SAC, the B-58s were sold for salvage in 1977. Two years later there were no Hustler airframes left at Davis Monthan. (Author's Collection)

This once proud B-52E (57-0101) served with the 96th Bomb Wing. This August 1976 photo shows her lying in the boneyard. (Author's Collection)

SAC's once majestic "Big Sticks" now sit forlorn and forgotten, awaiting the cutter's axe at Davis Monthan. (Author's Collection)

In 1971 all the B-52Cs and some of the B-52Fs were phased out of SAC's inventory. (Ethell)

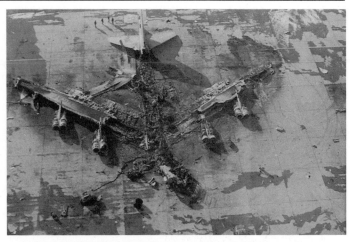

Disaster struck the flightline at Minot AFB, North Dakota on November 14, 1975. B-52H (61-0033) caught fire during ground refueling and burned. There were two fatalities. (5th BW/PAO)

B-52G (57-6515) prepares to take off from Beale AFB, California for a "Bullet Shot" deployment to Southeast Asia on April 15, 1972. (Ethell)

On April 9, 1972 B-52D (56-0665) landed at DaNang Air Base, South Vietnam with 156 holes caused by a near miss SAM detonation during a mission. She was repaired to fly more missions. (Ethell)

B-52D (55-0059) is loaded with a "clip" of bombs in preparation for another Linebacker mission to downtown Hanoi. (USAF)

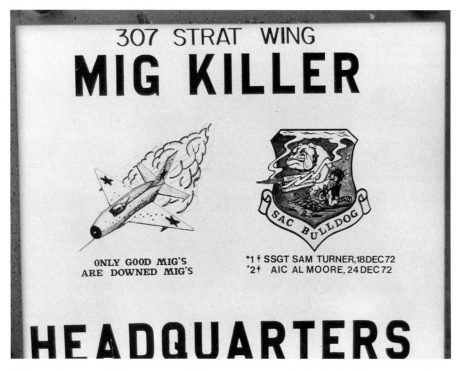

The 307th Strategic Wing put together this commemorative to celebrate the MiG kills by the BUFFs.

On June 22, 1973 B-52H (60-0061) was delivered to the 410th Bomb Wing at K.I. Sawyer AFB to become SAC's first BUFF with the new Electro Optical Viewing System (EVS). (Ethell)

The 380th Bomb Wing set an unprecedented record by winning the Fairchild Trophy four times for bombing/navigation. They took top honors in 1974, 1976, 1977, and 1978. No competition was held in 1975. (Burridge)

SAC used the T-39 as a command utility aircraft during the early 1970s. Most of these aircraft were transferred to the Military Airlift Command by 1975. (Joe Bruch Collection)

B-52G (57-6497) wears the crest of the 379th Bomb Wing in July 1979. (Burridge)

A thirsty SR-71 refuels from a KC-135Q during a sortie. Because of the difference in the fuel that the Blackbird uses, SAC had to maintain a dedicated fleet of tankers for the SR-71. (USAF)

B-52s staging out of Anderson AFB, Guam had a long over water flight to reach the target zone. (USAF)

The business end of the refueling boom on a KC-135 tanker at Minot during routine inspection. (5th BW/PAO)

RAPID RABBIT was one of four SR-71s to deploy to Kadena for operations in 1968. This aircraft was written off after a crash landing at Kadena in May 1973. (USAF)

A KC-135 refuels a B-52H during an Organizational Readiness Inspection. (USAF)

KC-135 (61-0270) was one of five tankers to be modified to serve as radio relay aircraft under the Combat Lighting program. The SAC sash has been removed in the 1973 photo taken at U-Tapao in 1973. (Joe Bruch Collection)

KC-135 (58-0074) was updated to KC-135Q standards and served with the dedicated SR-71 fleet at Beale AFB, California. (Joe Bruch Collection)

On February 3, 1973 the 55th Strategic Recon Wing at Offutt observed the passing of the 123,672nd accident-free operational hour of the Looking Glass. (Harris)

A minuteman missile is prepared for test launch at Vandenburg AFB. Periodically operational missiles are removed from alert silos and transported to Vandenburg to be fired. This random sampling helps assure that the missiles are ready in spite of storage in alert silos. (Felling)

This EC-135 (61-0261) is part of the COVER ALL airborne command post network. She was photographed while attached to the 305th Air Refueling Wing, May 1983. (Burridge)

A KC-10 (79-1710) from the 32nd Air Refueling Squadron/2nd Bomb Wing from Barksdale AFB, on the Andrews AFB ramp in May 1983. (Burridge)

5
1980s

The Strategic Air Command began the new decade by contributing units from the 57th Air Division to the newly formed Strategic Projection Force. The rationale behind this force was to maintain a part of the overall military in a ready condition in order to deal with a non-nuclear conventional crisis anywhere in the world.

In September, SAC tested its part of the Strategic Projection Force with Operation "Busy Prairie." B-52Hs from Minot deployed to Whiteman AFB, Missouri to act as a simulated forward operating base. B-52s from Grand Forks AFB flew from their home base on simulated missions. While the BUFFS were flying their missions to the Nevada ranges, SR-71s and EC-135s flew recon over simulated targets. As always, the ever present tankers supported the exercise.

The first Air Launched Cruise Missiles were delivered to the 416th Bomb Wing at Griffiss AFB, New York on January 11, 1981. The first missiles were used for training and testing under various operational conditions.

On March 17th the first KC-10 arrived at Barksdale AFB, The new tanker was based on the civilian DC-10 airframe and would provide SAC with updated tanker capabilities. The first aircraft was delivered by General Edgar S. Harris Jr, commander of the Eighth Air Force.

President Ronald Reagan announced the renewal of the B-1 program calling for one hundred airframes to be built and made operational as soon as possible. The President endorsed the development of the MX missile to replace the aging Titan II missiles that were then being phased out.

The Strategic Projection Force was tested again in November during Operation "Bright Star." B-52Hs from Minot and Grand Forks flew non-stop from their respective bases to a simulated target in Egypt to deliver their conventional bombs. The 31 hour mission was the longest mission to date for SAC aircraft.

Women have always been a vital part of the Strategic Air Command. On June 10, 1982 the first all female crew made a five hour training flight from Castle Air Force Base. The flight of "Fair Force

A U-2R from the 9th Strategic Recon Wing on the Andrews AFB flightline in May 1984. (Burridge)

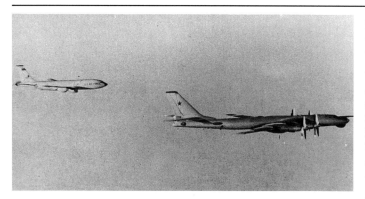

Fighter jocks were always intercepting Soviet Bear Bombers. Here a crew of Tanker Toads intercept a Bear off the coast of Iceland. (Watton)

One" was the first time that an all female crew had flown an actual mission.

The first KC-135R, an updated version of the regular SAC tanker, rolled out of the Boeing Plant at Wichita on June 22nd, and featured the more fuel efficient, and quieter, CFM-56 turbofan engines.

Under Project Rivet Cap, the deactivation of the Titan II complexes was begun. Liquid propellants used in the Titan brought several problems to the surface. Storage of these highly flammable materials posed danger to local storage facilities until it could be transported to Vandenberg for use in actual launches there. When the last Titan II was removed from their silos the age of liquid fueled missiles came to an end.

Secretary of the Air Force, Verne Orr announced that Dyess Air Force Base, Texas would become the first base to use the B-1B on January 31, 1983. The first unit to receive the new bomber would be the 96th Bomb Wing, and would be responsible for bringing the B-1B up to operational status along with training the crews to fly it.

As part of the collateral maritime mission handed to SAC, B-52Ds and B-52Gs from several wings took part in Team Spirit 83 during March. The B-52s were handed the task of mining a simulated target area off the coast of Korea. As part of Team Spirit a B-52G test fired a Harpoon missile down the Pacific Test Range.

The old warrior B-52D was removed from operations in October of 1983. To many who had worked on her and flew her into combat, she was the best B-52 ever built, and for several crew chiefs, she was *the* B-52. Anything with a shorter tail just happened to resemble the real thing. Due to its experience in combat and the fact that there were many examples available, B-52Ds went to many museums around the country. The last flying example left Carswell AFB on February 20, 1984 for display at Orlando's International Airport.

The first reengined KC-135R was delivered to the 384th Air Refueling Wing at McConnell AFB, Kansas on June 20, 1984. The updated versions of the old airframe workhorse would bring a new dimension to refueling operations.

September saw the Strategic Air Command participate in Gallant Eagle 84. This was the largest military war game held in the United States since 1962. This integrated exercise tested the ability of the entire military to coordinate activities during a time of national crisis. SAC B-52s flew over 182 sorties supported by over 309 tanker sorties.

September 4th saw the roll out of the first B-1B from the factory at Rockwell International. Those that attended the ceremony were impressed with the way the new bomber looked. The B-1B took to the air for the first time on October 18th.

The last of the E-4As that had undergone configuring to the E-4B was delivered to the 55th Strategic Recon Wing at Offutt on January 30, 1985. This marked the end of the update program for the National Emergency Airborne Command Post (NEACP) aircraft. The E-4B carried a more powerful generator along with new communications equipment and shielding from the effects of a nuclear blast.

On February 19th a B-52 from the 319th Bomb Wing at Grand Forks AFB, launched the first test ALCM over the Beufort Sea north of Canada. The test flight covered over 1,500 miles through the wilderness of Canada and made a parachute landing on target in the test range near Cold Lake, Alberta.

During the 1982 Bombing Navigation Competition, the 509th Bomb Wing set an unprecedented record by winning five major trophies. Here a 509th crew prepares their FB-111 for another training flight. (Harris)

A familiar landmark at Offutt AFB, Nebraska was removed on April 12th. The sign at the front gate proclaiming, PEACE IS OUR PROFESSION was taken down and donated to the SAC Aerospace Museum. The sign had stood at the front gate since 1958.

The 96th Bomb Wing at Dyess accepted the first B-1B on July 7th. The bomber arrived under a cloud of circumstances when the first scheduled aircraft (83-0065) suffered foreign object damage to an engine while at Omaha. The only other flyable B-1B (82-0001) was flown in to act as the ceremonial aircraft.

The famed SAC Looking Glass airborne command post celebrated twenty-five years of service on February 3, 1986. During that time there had been a Looking Gass in the air, around the clock, ready to take over command and control in the event that SAC Headquarters had been knocked out during a nuclear exchange.

Strategic Air Command turned forty on March 21st, and an impressive birthday cake was served at the Headquarters cafeteria. General Larry Welch, Commander in Chief, Strategic Air Command (CINCSAC) did the cake-cutting honors at the observance. While Headquarters celebrated the event, it was business as usual at the bases around the world. SAC may have turned forty, but it wasn't "over the hill."

The big news of 1987 was the B-1B. SAC's new manned bomber began breaking and setting records on April 14th. A B-1B from the 96th Bomb Wing set a new endurance record for that type of aircraft staying in the air for 13 hours and 20 minutes. Another record fell to the B-1B on the Fourth of July when a B-1B unofficially broke four world speed records for that class of aircraft.

Although it wasn't a record attempt, the B-1B chalked up the first Short Range Attack Missile launch on June 3rd. The test bore out the concept that that B-1B could indeed carry the SRAM.

Records continued to fall to the B-1B in September. A B-1B from Dyess set nine payload and speed records. While many of the records set by the new bomber were listed as unofficial, it didn't mean that the records had not been broken. It only indicated that the measuring equipment for "official" sanction had not been in place at the time of the attempt.

The controversy surrounding the B-1B was punctuated in 1988. The last example of the aircraft rolled out of the factory on January 20th, and this the 100th B-1B was destined for the 384th Bomb Wing at McConnell AFB, Kansas. With the final roll out the media continued to hammer at the aircraft's ability to complete its mission if called upon to do so. Disaster struck the B-1B fleet in No-

The TR-1A is used for tactical battlefield surveillance, high altitude standoff and weather surveillance. There were about 37 TR-1's under SAC's control. (Burridge)

vember with the crash of two of the multimillion dollar aircraft within eleven days. The first occurred at Dyess AFB, when a B-1B crashed on takeoff. The second crash was at Ellsworth AFB, South Dakota. In both cases the crews were able to eject from their aircraft. These back to back crashes set off the media bloodhounds.

The last year of the decade saw the Fifteenth Air Force participate in Operation "Giant Warrior." The thirty day exercise was the largest deployment in the Pacific area since 1975 and saw over 2,000 members of SAC deployed to various bases throughout the area. B-1Bs and B-52s dropped practice bombs on selected simulated targets while tankers supported the efforts.

The oldest B-52G, ELDERSHIP (58-0232), in SAC's inventory was retired at Offutt AFB on July 10, 1989. It entered service in 1959 and had flown combat in Southeast Asia, and made national news in 1987 when she was involved in a mid-air encounter with a bald eagle. Her service life over, she was placed on a stand to guard the main gate at Offutt.

The decade closed with the sphere of Communist influence shrinking on what seemed a daily basis. The Berlin Wall had crumbled. Soviet leadership no longer boasted, "We will bury you." They now wanted to open new line of economic trade and exchange.

The first TR-1A reached SAC's inventory on September 15, 1981. Most of the aircraft are stationed at RAF Alconbury, England. This example was photographed at Andrews AFB. (Burridge)

B-52H (60-0046) from the 7th Bomb Wing carries the name IRON BUTTERFLY. She carries very little fuel in the left wing as evidenced by the outrigger wheel that is so far off the ground in this May 1983 photo. (Burridge)

A B-52G (57-6518) with SRAMs on the underwing pylons. (Ethell)

This B-52D slides away from the tanker during Exercise Team Spirit 82 deployment to the Republic of Korea. (USAF)

A B-52H (60-0044) comes in for landing at Andrews AFB in May 1981. The BUFF was assigned to the 410th Bomb Wing at the time. (Burridge)

An interesting photo of a B-52G with her left wing damaged. At the present time we have no information as to the cause of this particular accident. (Author's Collection)

Coming in for a landing at Andrews AFB. This KC-135 (60-0326) is from the 379th Bomb Wing at Wurtsmith AFB, Michigan, May 1980. (Burridge)

SAC undertook a program to update the aging KC-135 fleet. With the new CFM-56 engines the KC-135R is quieter, faster and more fuel efficient. 61-0293 was photographed in May 1985 at Andrews AFB. (Burridge)

A B-52H from the 92nd Bomb Wing at Fairchild executes a missed approach at its home base in June 1989. (USAF)

SR-71 (64-17964) makes a low pass in review for the airshow crowd at Andrews AFB, May 1981. (Burridge)

She looks more like a Star Wars craft than a veteran of almost twenty-six years of service. This Blackbird (64-17964) was captured at Andrews AFB, May 1981. (Burridge)

SR-71 (64-17975) recovering from a training mission at its home base, Beale AFB, California, February 5, 1981. (Author's Collection)

The SR-71 was used for domestic recon as well as military. Two Blackbirds were used to photograph the destruction caused by the eruption of Mount St. Helens on May 18, 1980. (Author's Collection)

Blackbird (64-17972) set two world class records in 1974. She set both the Yew York to London record and the London to Los Angeles record of three hours forty-seven minutes 35.8 seconds. Photographed in May 1980, she still held the records. (USAF)

SR-71 (64-17979) taxies into the recovery area at Beale on February 12, 1981. (Author's Collection)

Wearing the shield of the 9th Strategic Recon Wing, #979 undergoes system checks in the recovery area on February 12, 1981. (Author's Collection)

Before going back into one of the bird cages at Beale AFB, a Blackbird recovers during the cool down period after a mission in February 1981. (Mayer)

SR-71 (64-17979) at Detachment 4 (Det 4) RAF Mildenhall on May 26, 1985. Mildenhall was the European staging base for the Blackbird. (Palmer)

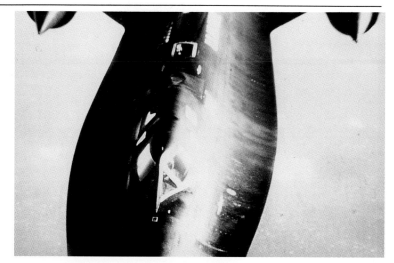

A Blackbird drops away from the tanker after taking on a load of JP-7. (Author's Collection)

SR-71 (64-17971) at a Fairchild AFB, Washington airshow May 18, 1980. (LaBouy)

Blackbird 64-17980 taxies out for a mission in 1982. On April 15, 1986 she flew post strike recon over Libya after Operation Eldorado Canyon. (Author's Collection)

SR-71 (64-17974) from the 9th Strategic Recon Wing at Beale AFB, May 1982. (Author's Collection)

Under threatening Nebraska skies, E-4B (85-0125) sits on the ramp at Offutt, AFB. (Author's Collection)

A E-4B National Emergency Airborne Command Post (NEACP) from the 55th Strategic Recon Wing on final approach to Offutt AFB, August 11, 1987. (Hill)

The concept of airborne control and post attack capabilities were proven on April 1, 1981. For the first time, a Minuteman III was launched from Vandenberg after receiving the launch signal code from an airborne E-4 command post. (Joe Bruch Collection)

The 55th Strategic Recon Wing took delivery of the first E-4B, like this one on January 11, 1980. (Joe Bruch Collection)

By January 1985, all E-4A's had been modified to E-4B configuration. The most noticeable change was the radome on top for satellite communications. (Joe Bruch Collection)

A "cocked" B-52H from the 5th Bomb Wing stands ready on the alert ramp at Minot AFB, North Dakota during the early 1980s. (Hill)

B-52Gs from the 319th Bomb Wing Grand Forks AFB, North Dakota, September 7, 1983. (Hill)

B-52G (57-6473) from the 93rd Bomb Wing at Castle AFB, California. She served as a test aircraft for the ill-fated Skybolt missile program. (Rogers)

B-52H (61-0034) of the 5th Bomb Wing on a low level practice bomb run October 14, 1987. (Hill)

B-52G (57-6512) pops her chute to slow her down after a mission. The open bomb bay is of interest. (USAF)

B-52H (60-0025) was the first B-52 to arrive at Minot AFB. Assigned to the 4136th Strategic Wing on July 13, 1961, she was back at Minot serving with the 5th Bomb Wing on September 22, 1987. (Hill)

In the early Dakota morning, a BUFF hits the runway during a GLOBAL SHIELD MITO. (Brenner)

0701 Hours, June 15, 1986, SAC launches the final phase of GLOBAL SHIELD 86. Two B-52Hs are already in the air while two are rolling on the runway during a Minimum Interval Take Off. (MITO). (Hill)

B-52s like this one on the alert pad at Minot AFB, North Dakota, stood armed and ready in any kind of weather— from freezing cold to summer thunderstorms. (USAF)

A 416th Bomb Wing B-52G armed with Air Launched Cruise Missiles (ALCM). The 416th was the first wing to become operational with the ALCM in December 1982. (USAF)

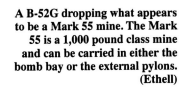

A B-52G dropping what appears to be a Mark 55 mine. The Mark 55 is a 1,000 pound class mine and can be carried in either the bomb bay or the external pylons. (Ethell)

SAC began retiring many of the high airframe time B-52G's in the late 1980's. (Ethell)

BUFFS on the flightline at Minot in the mid-1980s. (Pietsch)

**B-52H (61-0029) from the 5th Bomb Wing formates with a LOOKING GLASS EC-135
during a mission over the frozen Canadian tundra. (Ethell)**

B-52H (60-0015) carries the crest of the 7th Bomb Wing from Carswell AFB, Texas. (Author's Collection)

BUFFs and tankers refuel in a cell on the way to their "Fail Safe" Positive Control Point. Unless they receive the correct "Go Code" they will return to their base. (Nash)

As part of the Strategic Projection Force the B-52H can carry a wide range of conventional weapons. (Hill)

B-52H (61-0031) from the 92nd Bomb Wing carries the Seahawk insignia from Fairchild AFB on her tail in this December 1988 photo. (Hill)

B-52H (60-0007) known as "Dak Rat" approaches Minot AFB after a training sortie on September 21, 1989. (Hill)

B-52H, alias OPUS, executes a missed approach at Minot, AFB October 5, 1989. (Hill)

B-52H (61-0023) SOD BUSTER sits cocked and ready on the alert ramp at Minot in August 1989. (Rogers)

SOD BUSTER from the 5th Bomb Wing photographed at Ellsworth AFB during a visit to Rapid City in October 1989. (Rogers)

B-52H (61-0027) LAND SCRAPPER II from the 7th Bomb Wing on the ramp at Carswell AFB, Texas, in late 1989. (Rogers)

Somewhere over the rainbow happens to be Anderson AFB, Guam, in this early 1980s photo. (Amundson)

During a MITO a lot of JP-4 is converted into noise and clouds of dense black smoke. (Brenner)

Looking Glass from the 55th Strategic Recon Wing at Offutt celebrated the 20th Anniversary on February 3, 1981. In that twenty years the 55th had flown 195,401 continuous airborne command post flying hours. (Author's Collection)

This EC-135 (63-8001) from the 28th Bomb Wing is open to the public at Friends and Neighbors open house at Grand Forks AFB. (Hill)

DINA MIGHT a EC-135 from the 28th Bomb Wing, on display at Minot AFB, August 20, 1989 (Hill)

A KC-135 (60-0326) from the 379th Bomb Wing stationed at Wurtsmith AFB, Michigan on the ramp at Andrews AFB, May 10, 1980. (Miller)

KC-135 (56-3656) from the 7th Bomb Wing on the take off roll from Carswell AFB, Texas, October 25, 1980. (Author's Collection)

A KC-135 (61-0310) from the 384th Air Refueling Wing, May 18, 1980. Six months later, the 384th won the 1980 Saunders Trophy as the best tanker unit in SAC. (Author's collection)

KC-135s from the New Hampshire Air National Guard on the flightline at Anderson AFB, Guam, in the early 1980s. (Amundson)

This KC-135 from the 97th Bomb Wing was displayed at an open house at Blytheville, Arkansas in the early 1980s. (Author's Collection)

KC-135 (56-3640) from the 132nd Air Refueling Squadron, Maine Air National Guard transient to Forbes AFB, Kansas, in January 1981. (USAF)

KC-135s from the 905th
Air Refueling Squadron
on the line at Grand
Forks AFB, North
Dakota, September 7,
1983. (Hill)

KC-135 (57-1490) of the
7th Bomb Wing taxies out
for a refueling mission on
August 21, 1981.
(Swendrowski)

Her mission complete
KC-135 63-8021 comes
home to roost at Minot
on October 14, 1987.
(Hill)

KC-135 (62-3525) was assigned to the 305th Air Refueling Wing at Grissom AFB, Indiana. (Truax)

This KC-135 (63-7987) carries the rainbow tail markings of the 410th Bomb Wing at K.I. Sawyer AFB, Michigan. (Traux)

In the late 1980s SAC repainted the KC-135 fleet to make them less visible for potential hostile fighters. THE MAGIC CARPET (56-3620) was photographed at Minot. (Hill)

KC-135 (56-3620) at the Minot International Airport.

KC-135A (59-1449) from the 307th Air Refueling Squadron attached to the 410th Bomb Wing at K.I. Sawyer AFB, Michigan, in July 1981. (Love)

A KC-135A (63-8005) from the 71st Air Refueling Squadron stationed at Barksdale AFB. (Truax)

KC-135A (57-1483) from the 340th Air Refueling Group on the rain soaked flightline at Altus AFB, Oklahoma, April 18, 1981. (Author's Collection)

KC-135A (62-3554) from the 905th Air Refueling Squadron and her mates grace the flightline at Grand Forks AFB during the mid 1980s. (Hill)

KC-135 (61-0280) at Mildenhall RAF, UK on April 12, 1985. (Palmer)

KC-135Q (58-0054) undergoes repair of the number 1 engine at Beale AFB. (Mayer)

KC-135Q (58-0071) sports the new grey paint job while her 9th Strategic Recon Wing ramp mates still have the aluminum paint, in this February 1981 photo. (Author's Collection)

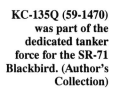

KC-135Q (59-1470) was part of the dedicated tanker force for the SR-71 Blackbird. (Author's Collection)

The 319th Bomb Wing received their first updated KC-135R in the fall of 1987. KC-135R 62-3537 sits on the flight line at Grand Forks waiting for "Friends and Neighbors" June 25, 1988. (Hill)

A 384th Bomb Wing KC-135R leaves McConnell for a mission. In November 1988, four KC-135Rs from different wings established four world records for their class of aircraft. (Boeing)

KC-135R (59-1459) wears the unit crest of the 28th Bomb Wing. (Hill)

This KC-135R carries the shield of the 384th Bomb Wing from McConnell AFB near Wichita, Kansas. (Author's Collection)

The first KC-135R (61-0293) with the updated CFM-56 engines was delivered to the 384th Air Refueling Wing at McConnell AFB, Kansas on June 20, 1984. (Rued)

RC-135U (64-14847) from the 55th Strategic Recon Wing at Offutt AFB, Nebraska, July 13, 1981. (Author's Collection)

Another view of #847 shows that she is undergoing an engine change on number 2 in this July 13, 1981 photo. (Author's Collection)

RC-135V (64-14844) on the Offutt ramp in July 1981. She started her career as a RC-135C and was later updated to present configuration. (Author's Collection)

RC-135V (64-14841) at Offutt on June 12, 1981. The mission of the recon 135 is to gather information on possible foes around the world. Needless to say, the actual mission profile is classified. (Author's Collection)

RC-135V (63-9792) from the 55th Strategic Recon Wing at Offutt, June 12, 1981. (Author's Collection)

The 55th Strategic Recon Wing maintains SAC's RC-135 fleet. Here a RC-135W returns to Offutt after a mission on August 11, 1987.

High over the northern Pacific a COBRA BALL takes on a fuel load. Note the flat black paint on the right wing. (Amundson)

The first B-1B, 83-0065, was delivered on June 29, 1985. The only other B-1B at the time was 82-0001. She was delivered to the 96th Bomb Wing at Dyess AFB, Texas and became LEADER OF THE FLEET as depicted here in service with the 28th Bomb Wing at Rapid City, (Rogers)

B-1B (85-0089) MIDNIGHT PROWLER from the 28th Bomb Wing at Ellsworth in May 1989. (Rogers)

PROUD SHIELD 89 was the second appearance of the B-1B in the SAC bombing competition. The 28th Bomb Wing-Black Hills Bandits brought the Fairchild Trophy home to Ellsworth. (Rogers)

Wings back, a B-1B from Ellsworth shows the troops at Minot just what the big dark bird will do at low level. (Hill)

The 28th Bomb Wing was the second unit to receive the B-1B. They took delivery of their first aircraft on January 21, 1987. (Hill)

B-1B (86-0103) from the 28th Bomb Wing departs from Minot after a weekend airshow, August 21, 1989. (Hill)

B-1B (86-0105) from the 28th Bomb Wing during final approach to Minot AFB, November 13, 1987. (Hill)

During a routine training flight, the nosewheel failed to extend during approach for landing. After five hours of flight, including diverting to Edwards AFB, the crew brought the crippled Lancer in for a landing. (USAF)

Trailing a rooster tail of dust, Captain Jeff Bean brings his aircraft in for an emergency landing on October 4, 1989. (USAF)

Sandblasted and scrapped, EXCALIBUR (85-0070) sits on the dry lake after her epic emergency landing. (USAF)

SPECTRE (86-0109) taxies out for a night training mission at Ellsworth AFB, South Dakota (28th BW).

A B-1B from the 28th Bomb Wing at Ellsworth, banks for the camera over the South Dakota Countryside. (28th BW)

The prototype KC-10 refuels the first KC-10 to be delivered to SAC. The first delivery took place on March 17, 1981 to the 2nd Bomb Wing at Barksale AFB. (McDonald/Douglas)

This KC-10 from March AFB shows off the dark paint of the late 1980s. (Hill)

Above: A KC-10 from Barksdale AFB, pulls up to a roving KC-135 for a refill. (Watton)

Below: Inflight refueling capability of the KC-10 allows it to refill from another tanker and continue the mission. (Watton)

Since April 1976, SAC has been a participant in the RED FLAG program at Nellis AFB, Nevada. (Brenner)

KC-135s can be fitted with hose refueling system to refuel Navy aircraft like this EA-6B Prowler. (Brenner)

Above: A 509th Bomb Wing FB-111 holds in a pre-contact stable position before moving in for the hook up. (Brenner)

Below: "Contact!" Within seconds the fuel will be filling the tanks and the FB-111 will continue on the mission. (Brenner)

Rehearsal for Armageddon. Three Minuteman warheads streak across the sky towards impact in the test area. (Jenkins)

The first MX Peacekeeper was launched from Vandenberg on June 18, 1983. The Peacekeeper was a follow on ICBM to the aging Minuteman system. (USAF)

Workdays in SAC ran on a twenty-four hour clock. Munitions crew uploads a rack of AGM-86B cruise missiles under the lights. (Ethell)

Ellsworth AFB, South Dakota was the host base for the 1985 Weapons loading Competition, September 19-26, 1985. (USAF)

The Barrentine Trophy for Best Munitions Competition Team went to this team from the 509th Bomb Wing. (USAF)

The 509th also won the Best Munitions Load Crew and Best Combined Load Crew awards. (USAF)

A KC-135R quenches the thirst of three Tomcats during a Desert Storm mission. (Campbell Archives/OKC)

6
1990s

The Strategic Air Command entered the 1990s with a feeling of uncertainty regarding its future. There were rumblings coming from the Pentagon about possible restructuring of the military.

Undaunted by the rumor mongers, SAC continued with the day to day business of training, keeping the birds ready to fly and maintaining a strong alert posture.

On January 18th the legendary SR-71 Blackbird completed the final operational mission at Kadena AFB, Okinawa. Kadena was the first overseas base to become operational with the Blackbird. It was only fitting that it became the first base outside the United States to end Blackbird recon flights.

The last Blackbird to retire was to be placed on display in Washington D.C. To prove that the old bird still had it in her, a new record was set during the flight from the West Coast to Dulles International Airport. Old 972 was the same Blackbird that had set a New York to London record. With retirement of the Blackbird there were many requests from various museums to obtain an example of the aircraft for display.

As the Soviet Union continued to shrink, the Pentagon announced more and more cutbacks in military spending. One of the first items to get the axe was the B-2 Stealth bomber. Originally proposed as a replacement for the B-52 fleet, it had undergone cutbacks before, but the very survival of the aircraft seemed to be threatened.

On July 24, 1990 the EC-135 LOOKING GLASS stood down from airborne alert marking the end of an era. For the first time in many years there would be no LOOKING GLASS in the air in the event of a national emergency. The EC-135s would now maintain a ground alert posture.

On July 24, 1990 the EC-135 LOOKING GLASS stood down from airborne alert. From that day forward they maintained a 15 minute ground alert. (USAF)

Moments After the Klaxon goes off, SAC aircraft are headed for the active runway during a practice alert. (Nash)

While the Soviet Union may have been in a state of collapse, trouble was brewing in the Middle East. Military forces from Iraq had invaded that small oil rich country of Kuwait. The United Nations formed a coalition demanding that the Iraq withdraw. It looked as if the United States would bear the brunt of supplying men and arms to take on this new, so called "world bully."

During the build up in the Middle East, SAC tankers flew countless refueling missions in support of the movement of fighters from the United States to Saudi Arabia. The tankers also provided refueling to transports that were airlifting everything needed for a sustained campaign in the Middle East. Without the aerial refueling capabilities provided by the Strategic Air Command it would have been impossible to mount a campaign on the other side of the world in such a short time frame.

The air offensive against Iraq started in the early hours of January 16, 1991. The opening blows were thrown by F-117 Stealth fighters. SAC tankers were there, as always, ready to keep the thirsty fighters topped off with JP-4. A flight of B-52Gs had secretly left Barksdale AFB the day before and headed east towards the Gulf. When they reached their launch points they fired the first conventional warhead armed ALCMs at targets within Iraq. After a round trip of over 34 hours, the BUFFs landed back at Barksdale. What the flight crews called "Secret Squirrel" would go into the books not only as a successful mission, but also as the longest combat mission in the history of the U.S. Air Force.

What was supposed to be the *mother of all wars* turned out to be the mother of all pastings. Aircraft pounded Iraqi forces day and night. SAC B-52s pounded the supposedly elite Republican Guard from both high and low altitude during the air offensive. While the "Bomber Pukes" were hitting their targets, the "Tanker Toads" were just as busy flying their endless racetracks in the sky above Middle East. As before in combat and peacetime, the tankers were there when they were needed adding more saves to a legacy that had grown out of Viet Nam.

The complete economic collapse of the Soviet Union brought about feelings that we as a nation had not experienced since the end of World War II. The threat of nuclear holocaust was lower then it had ever been. Peace was at hand. The Cold War was over.

On September 28, 1991 by order of the President of the United States, George Bush, the Strategic Air Command stood down from fifteen minute ground alert. Across the country, alert crews gathered their equipment from the alert facility and prepared to relax. Out on the ramp, ground crews were busy downloading the weapons from the aircraft. For the first time since October 1, 1957, the Strategic Air Command had no aircraft on ground alert.

An interesting sidelight to the stand down was the closing of the actual alert facility. Under orders handed down, the building was to be locked. Since the building had to be open at any given moment, there had not been locks installed on many of the facilities. Thus, locks had to be procured and installed to comply with the orders.

While the bomber crews stood down from alert, the missilemen maintained a standby alert posture. Although their posture was relaxed to a certain degree, they remained ready with *pointed end up and everything in the green.*

On June 1, 1992 the Strategic Air Command became a part of our nations past military history. As part of the restructuring of the Air Force, Strategic Air Command combined with Tactical Air Command to become Air Combat Command. The assets of the command would be divided between ACC and the newly formed Air Mobility Command.

The mailed fist of the Strategic Air Command stood ready to hurl the lightning bolts of destruction from its grasp for forty six years. In the end, the constant readiness to destroy brought forth the olive branch of peace. The men and women who served in the Strategic Air Command are the victors of the Cold War. PEACE IS OUR PROFESSION was not only their motto, PEACE WAS THEIR PRODUCT!!

A B-52H carrying a full load of ALCMs lands at Minot. The ALCM has an approximate range of 1500 miles. (Nash)

PHOENIX (85-0088) of the 28th Bomb Wing ready for a training mission in April 1990. (Rogers)

The graceful lines of the B-1B show up against a solid undercast. The boomer has just shaken the bomber off the boom after refueling. (Watton)

THOR (85-0091) carries a big hammer plus a lot more for the 28th Bomb Wing. (Rogers)

After the bomber force stood down, only SAC's missiles remained as a alert ready nuclear strike force. (USAF)

The first Peacekeepers to reach SAC units were to be housed in silos. The rail garrison concept was deemed too expensive for future use. (USAF)

Dark and dangerous, KNIGHT WARRIOR of the 5th Bomb Wing uses a mountain pass to hide from radar as she practices penetration techniques. (Forsberg)

At least one of the E-4B aircraft remains on station alert at Washington D.C., ready to carry the President into the air during a national crisis. (Author's Collection)

A KC-135 from the 906th Air Refueling Squadron leaves Minot for the other side of the world during support operations for Desert Storm. (Hill)

High over the Atlantic a KC-135 refuels a C-141 Starlifter during deployment of troops for Operation Desert Shield. (Author's Collection)

High above the mid-west, a LOOKING GLASS takes on a load of fuel from a KC-135 tanker. (Brenner)

High above the desert an AWACS pulls into the pre contact stable position behind a SAC tanker. (Rassier)

During Operation Desert Storm, SAC tankers flew thousands of sorties to keep the fighters on station. (Rassier)

High over the fields of North Dakota, a F-117 Stealth fighter approaches a KC-135 from the 906th Air Refueling Squadron for a refueling hook up. (Watton)

The F-117 Stealth fighters were the spearhead for Desert Storm. SAC tankers were there to assure plenty of JP-4 for the thirsty fighters. (USAF)

B-52s flew numerous missions against the Republican Guard. The elite troops were pounded day and night with conventional bombs. By the time the ground war began, the Iraqi elite surrendered by the thousands. (Campbell Archives/OKC)

The 416th Bomb Wing deployed some of their B-52Gs to the Arabian Peninsula to fly combat missions during Desert Storm. (416th BW/PAO)

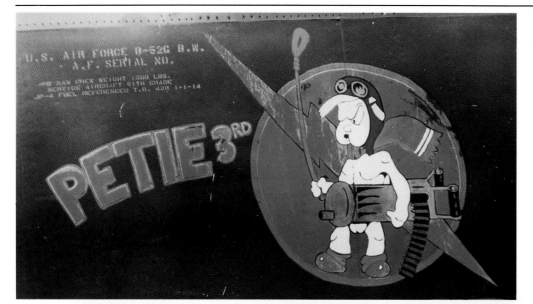

On January 16, 1991 B-52s from the 2nd Bomb Wing left their home base at Barksdale and headed for targets in Iraq. B-52G (58-0177) known as PETIE 3rd was the lead aircraft. (8th AF Museum)

GRIM REAPER (59-2582) flew the second position for the mission that would become known as "Secret Squirrel." (8th AF Museum)

MIAMI CLIPPER (57-6475) flew in the fourth position in the 35 hour plus mission to start Operation Desert Storm. (8th AF Museum)

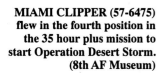

The "Secret Squirrel" mission marked the first launch of a conventional Air Launched Cruise Missile in combat. MISS FIT II (58-0238) flew in the fifth position. (8th AF Museum)

VALKYRIE (58-0183) flew in the sixth position of "Secret Squirrel." The aircrews that flew the mission were awarded the Air Medal. (8th AF Museum)

OLD CROW EXPRESS from the 379th Bomb Wing flew fifty-three missions during Operation Desert Storm. (Campbell Archives/OKC)

During Operation Desert Storm, Air National Guard and Reserve KC-135s supported the strike force. KC-135 #1438 from the 434th Air Refueling Wing sports 21 mission markings for service in the desert. (Campbell Archives/OKC)

CAMP NACIREMA, on the Arabian Peninsula. Nacirema is American spelled backwards. (416th BW/PAO)

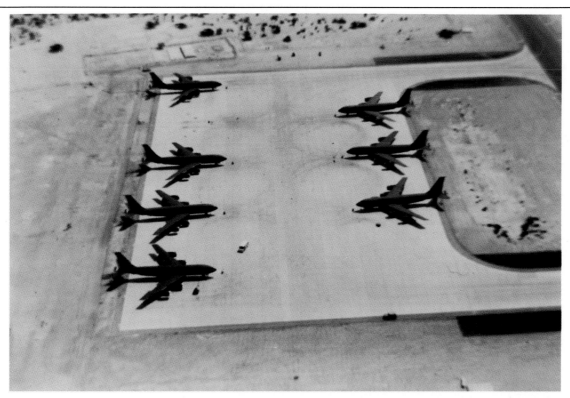

416th Bomb Wing KC-135s on the ramp at a base in Saudi Arabia during Operation Desert Storm. (416th BW/ PAO)

Tent city at CAMP NACIREMA during the desert war. This was the home of the 1702 nd Air Refueling Wing(P). (416th BW/PAO)

On September 30, 1991 the last B-52 mission with a tail gunner as part of the crew was flown by the 5th Bomb Wing. The crew posed after the historic flight. (5th BW/PAO)

In 1991, SAC's tail gunners were no longer needed to man the remote defenses. Here the last tail gunners from the 5th Bomb Wing gather for a group portrait. (5th BW/PAO)

Smoke and a ball of fire signal the launch of a Minuteman III from Vandenberg AFB, California. (McDowell)

The Minuteman leaves a trail of smoke through the California skies in mute evidence of her flight. (McDowell)

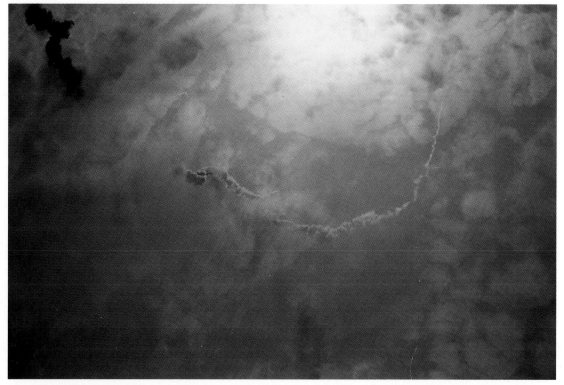

The solid fueled ICBM rolls out over the ocean headed down range towards the target during a Follow On Operational Test (FOOT). (McDowell)

With the collapse of the Soviet Union, the threat of global holocaust diminished. (5th BW/PAO)

Crews prepare to download the ALCMs from the alert ready B-52H at Minot Air Force Base. (5th BW/PAO)

A rack of ALCMs is pulled away from B-52H 61-0006 during the down loading of alert aircraft. (5th BW/PAO)

Trucks prepare to move the weapons from the alert ramp to the secure storage area. (5th BW/PAO)

After almost thirty years of fifteen minute ground alert, SAC was standing down. B-52H (61-0006) sits on the ramp after down loading of weapons was completed. Soon she would join her sister ships on the regular flightline at Minot AFB North Dakota. (5th BW/PAO)

On September 28, 1991, the Strategic Air Command received orders from the President to stand down from 15 minute ground alert. Above, a 5th Bomb Wing flightcrew removes their equipment from a B-52H on the alert pad. (5th BW/PAO)

Members of the groundcrew roll a weapons transporter into position below the bomb bay of an alert B-52H in preparation to down load the weapons. (5th BW/PAO)

B-1B AMERICAN MAID from the 319th Bomb Wing at Grand Forks AFB. (Hill)

B-52H (60-0029) comes in for a landing after a routine training flight. (Hill)

Even with the pressure of ground alert removed, down loading the weapons is done by the book. (5th BW/PAO)

With the weapons secured, the transporter will be removed from under the B-52. (5th BW/PAO)

A KC-10 from Barksdale AFB, makes a landing approach at Minot for the annual summer airshow. (Hill)

Under cloudy skies this U-2R (60-1094) from the 9th Strategic Recon Wing awaits the public during Northern Neighbors day at Minot. (Hill)

Sporting her last tail code variation for the Strategic Air Command, 60-0022 awaits the final days of her service to the mailed fist. (Hill)

About fifteen minutes after launch, three individual warheads streak across the sky in the target area. (USAF)

On June 1, 1992 the Strategic Air Command flew into history as it was combined with Tactical Air Command to form Air Combat Command. (Hill)

The crew of LINCOLN IMP during the 28th Bomb Group's deployment to RAF Scrampton, August 1948. (28th BW/PAO).

To the men 91st Strategic Recon Squadron she was AH SOOOOO. She was officially listed as 44-61817. (Moffitt)

ACE IN THE HOLE (44-61872) from the 98th Bomb Group. When she first arrived over Korea she was known as SAC'S APPEAL. (Campbell Archives/OKC)

RB-29A 44-61727 was named SO TIRED-SEVEN TO SEVEN and flew with the 91st Strategic Recon Squadron out of Yakota during the Korean War. (Moffitt)

B-29 #2253 from the 98th Bomb Group, Yakota AFB, Japan. (Campbell Archives/OKC)

TIGER LIL of the 91st Strategic Recon Squadron after 21 photo sessions over Korea. (Moffitt)

7
SAC ART

Historically, artwork on military aircraft had been around since World War I. Noseart as it became known, reached its high point during World War II when nearly every airplane had some kind of personal marking on it. After all, those huge aluminum spaces made natural canvases to display the crew's thoughts about those they had left behind back home.

In the post-war Air Force, nose art was not sanctioned according to regulations, as a result, it was not tolerated in most cases. The Strategic Air Command showed an early intolerance which bordered on downright disdain for anything associated with noseart. There were isolated examples of so called noseart on SAC aircraft, though in most cases it was a simple name on the side of the airplane, usually of the city where the aircraft was stationed.

When the men of SAC left the confines of stateside command and control for the skies above Korea, artwork began appearing on

their aircraft. Needless to say, men will be men, and many B-29s carried the usual beautiful tributes to the female form. Since most of the aircraft were stationed in Japan or Okinawa it didn't take long for someone to complain about the vulgarity associated with the artwork. In most cases swim suits were hastily applied or just the word "Censored" placed over strategic areas.

When the war in Korea ended so did the excuse for noseart. Aircraft that returned to the states with examples of noseart were quickly sanitized to conform with the watchful eyes of SAC's version of big brother.

For years, unofficial sanction was given to applying names to the sides of aircraft that were headed towards the annual bombing competition. It was felt that a name helped bolster the competitive spirit of SAC's World Series of Bombing. About the only other form of artwork tolerated was a cryptic name applied to the first aircraft to be assigned to a unit. Thus, there was the CITY OF ROME,

RB-29 (44-61951) better known as OUR L'LASS, served with the 91st Strategic Recon Squadron during Korea. (Moffitt)

The left side of OUR L'LASS sports the 91st insignia and her mission score. The large camera represents 50 missions to Korea. (Moffitt)

PEACE PERSUADER and MOHAWK VALLEY. Even these examples faded when the aircraft was transferred to another base or went through the modification depot.

Artwork had a brief rebirth during the war in Viet Nam. It was unofficial and unsanctioned. B-52s operating from Anderson AFB, Guam carried names like MEKONG EXPRESS, CHAIN OF THUNDER and CASPER. It didn't take long for the long arm of SAC to reach across the Pacific and inform the troops that names on aircraft would not be tolerated. It seemed that someone in the highs halls of the Pentagon was of the impression that painting names on the sides of aircraft would interfere with the effectiveness of the camouflage paint. The Paris Peace Accords not only ended the war in Viet Nam, it also put an end to the excuse to paint artwork on the sides of airplanes.

RB-29 (44-61948) THE GYPSY served with the 91st Strategic Recon Squadron at Yakota Japan during the Korean war. (Moffitt)

In the mid-1970s a strange thing started to happen. Names other then the crew chief started appearing in the little block on the sides of B-52s and KC-135s around the country. While the crew chief and his/her assistant were still listed, in many cases a short name appeared above the ground crew name. Thus there were examples of DEATH BY MAMBA, LITTLE JOE, and H.R. BUFFENSTUFF.

It was also during the 1970s that the Air Force initiated *Project Warrior* to increase the awareness of the past heritage. Since noseart was part of the past heritage and glory of the Air Force it was only natural that modernized versions of nose art began appearing on SAC aircraft.

The Air National Guard units paved the way with tail stripes painted on the tails of their KC-135s. Shortly, special artwork began appearing on some FB-111s at Pease AFB, New Hampshire. Most of the artwork was frequented back to those that had appeared on aircraft during World War II. This was deemed acceptable since it was inspired by past heritage and came under part of *Project Warrior.*

By 1988, CINCSAC, General John T. Chain Jr. jumped on the band wagon and revised SAC regulations to allow nose art to be placed on aircraft as long as it was done in subdued colors. With official sanction the nose art program needed a name. Nose art on SAC aircraft now came under the title *"Glossy Eagle."*

HONEYBUCKET HONSHOS from the 91st Strategic Recon Squadron at Yakota. Her official serial number was 44-61929. (Moffitt)

As nose art increased, troop morale rose like an eagle. Instead of referring to B-52H 60-0007 as Balls 7, it was now known as DAK RAT. Aircraft took on an individual character rather then just a number on the flightline.

It didn't take long for the press to get a hold of the fact that nose art was adorning the sides of B-52s and KC-135s at SAC bases around the country. With the publication of several photos, the battle lines were drawn.

Feminists proclaimed with anger that it was degrading to have the female form on aircraft that were supported by their tax dollars. Other groups complained that it was against motherhood to have women painted on the side of an aircraft that may have to take thousands of lives during a nuclear confrontation.

Out on the flightline the troops could have cared less about the growing flap over nose art. To most of them it was a great morale booster. What wasn't known or perhaps cared about by the opposing camp was the fact that each example of nose art had to go before a committee for approval. In most cases female officers were part of the committee. As a matter of fact, in several cases the artwork was applied by women artists. There were many reasons that artwork may not get the final approval. Take for example, SHEER

T.D.Y. WIDOW from the 98th. The name suggests a hopeful quick end to the tour of duty in Korea. (Campbell Archives/OKC)

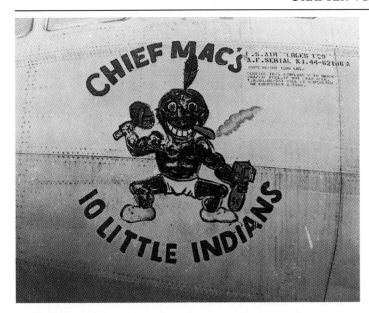

CHIEF MAC'S 10 LITTLE INDIANS served with the 98th Bomb Group during Korea. (Campbell Archives/OKC)

DESTRUCTION from the 5th Bomb Wing. At first it was felt that the somewhat "punk rock" hairdo of the lady would be more objectionable then the rather sheer clothing that covered her.

Detractors proclaimed that the artwork would be removed at once if the figure was a semi-nude man on the nose of the aircraft. A quick look through the nose art files will bring into view such examples as KNIGHT WARRIOR, THOR, and DRAGON SLAYER. All of which carry an example of the male form. So much for that particular argument.

It must be pointed out that not all art work was a 'degrading' painting of the female form. The are many examples of non-gender artwork in the nose art files. Yet, since it was nose art, it was considered to be degrading in some strange abstract form or another.

It didn't take long for the feminist movement to enlist the help of their lobbyist connection in Washington. Pressure was exerted on the Pentagon by several female members of Congress and at least one former female Vice Presidential Candidate to have the art work removed and the practice stopped once and for all.

It was a sad day, when the directive came down from the high halls of the Pentagon that gender related nose art would not be tolerated. The impact on morale was immediate and profound. Many felt that those members of the feminist movement that had yelled the loudest about how degrading the artwork was, were actually jealous. It was and still is felt by many that if the female contingent in the Congress would put as much effort into the budget or fighting drugs on our streets as they did in the nose art war, we would have clear streets and a lower deficit.

With the change of command and the passing of the Strategic Air Command into history, the feminist victory against nose art is complete. Under the new command of Air Combat Command the former SAC aircraft were sanitized to conform with the beliefs of the new command and control at Langley.

Gone are the days when beautiful artwork adorned the nose area of the bombers and tankers. Gone is the boost to morale of those who manned the flightdecks or kept them ready to fly. With the dawn of peace it is doubtful that we will see a resurgence of nose art in the near future. It is sad since it had really just gotten a good start at a comeback. Those of use who took the time to photograph these examples of Americana will have something to look back at from time to time and share with others in projects such as this.

Would *Glossy Eagle* have had a better chance if some feminist would have been the person standing guard on a frozen flightline. Would there have been a different attitude if instead of campaigning for office they would have been sweltering under the hot sun. Would it have been different if one of the things that reminded them of what they had left behind to defend, was the smile of the artwork looking down on them from a bomber or tanker. Would it have made a difference if the feminist movement was standing alert, ready to defend their country and their right to complain about something.

Would it have been . . . NAAAAH!!

MISS MINOOKI from the 98th. (Campbell Archives/OKC)

Without the name SHEER DESTRUCTION, 003 would be known as Balls 3 to the crews of the 5th Bomb Wing. (Hill)

NIP ON NEES was an interesting play on words no matter which way it was taken. She served with the 98th. (Campbell Archives/OKC)

The 99th Bomb Wing at Westover AFB, Mass was the second unit to receive the B-52. THE BIG STICK carried serial number 54-2673. (Burridge)

Door art on FB-111, 69-6513 of the 509th Bomb Wing traces the wings heritage back to the Second World War. (Burridge)

This artwork on FB-111 67-7196 commemorates the B-25 RUPTURED DUCK flown by Capt Ted Lawson's crew during the Doolittle Raid to Tokyo in April, 1942. (Burridge)

LAND SCRAPER II from the 7th Bomb Wing carries serial number 61-0027. (Rogers)

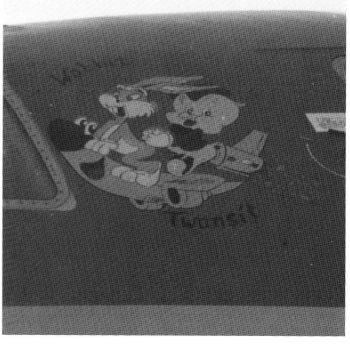

WABBIT TWANSIT, a KC-10A (79-1949) from the 22nd Air Refueling Wing at March AFB, California. (Burridge)

KNIGHT WARRIOR (60-0057) from the 5th Bomb Wing, Minot
AFB. (Hill)

B-52H (61-0011) BUFF RIDER stationed at Minot with the 5th
Bomb Wing. (Hill)

THE BARON traces the name back to World War II when the 5th
Bomb Wing was nicknamed "The Bomber Barons." (Hill)

B-52H 61-0023 was known as SOD BUSTER to the men of the 5th
Bomb Wing. The is one of the lowest flight time airframes in the B-
52 fleet. (Rogers)

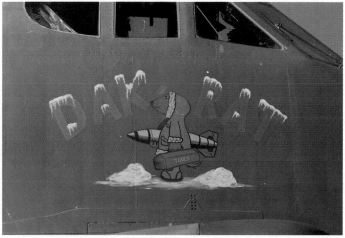

A very appropriate name for a B-52H. AGED TO PERFECTION
serves with the 5th Bomb Wing. (Hill)

Named after a local ground squirrel, DAK RAT was photographed
at Minot AFB, December 1, 1989. (Hill)

The first B-52H (60-0001) carried the name BLACK MAGIC II at Minot. (Hill)

SURPRISE ATTACK (60-0036) photographed on a cold and windy flight line at Minot, December 1, 1989. (Hill)

B-52G 59-2584 from the 93rd Bomb Wing carried the name MIDNIGHT EXPRESS. (Veronico)

B-52D CALAMITY JANE flew her share of missions over North Viet Nam. She is preserved at Mobile Alabama. (Campbell Archives/ OKC)

FB-111A (68-0289) from the 380th Bomb Wing at Plattsburgh AFB carries the name QUEEN HI in honor of a World War II B-24 from the 380th. (Hill)

B-52H (60-0043) from the 410th Bomb Wing. She was also known as BRIDESMAID BECKY. (Rogers)

FB-111A (68-0255) SLEEPY TIME GAL from the 380th Bomb Wing. (Campbell Archives/OKC)

MAD MAX, a KC-135R (62-3540) hailed from Ellsworth AFB, South Dakota, home of the 28th Bomb Wing. (Campbell Archives/OKC)

THE CONTENDER flew with the 93rd Bomb Wing. (Campbell Archives/OKC)

A tribute to Marilyn Monroe, KC-135R (62-3541) carries some impressive artwork in the form of NORMA JEAN. (Campbell Archives/OKC)

SKEETER EATER, KC-135R (60-0322) from the 19th Air Refueling Wing at Robins AFB, Georgia. (Campbell Archives/OKC)

SILVER SURFER (63-8034) served with the 906th Air Refueling Squadron at Minot. (Campbell Archives/OKC)

SOUTHERN BREEZE (63-8874) was updated to KC-135R standards and assigned to the 96th Bomb Wing. (Burridge)

CALIFORNIA OUTLAW (58-0125) from the 9th Strategic Recon Wing is a KC-135Q. (Burridge)

SWIFT HAWK from the 340th Air Refueling Wing at Altus AFB, Oklahoma. (Campbell Archives/OKC)

KC-135R (59-1517) HOOVER flies with the 28th Bomb Wing from Rapid City. (Burridge)

THE MAGIC CARPET (56-3620) of the 906th Air Refueling Squadron at Minot. (Hill)

WARLOCK WARRIOR (63-8006) from the 905th Air Refueling Squadron at Grand Forks AFB, North Dakota. (Campbell Archives/OKC)

ROLLING THUNDER an EC-135 from the 28th Bomb Wing. (Burridge)

GREY GHOST (59-1455) a KC-135R from the 28th Bomb Wing at Ellsworth AFB. (Campbell Archives/OKC)

THE OLD GREY HARE (57-1439) "Dedicated to the Memory of Hector Jimerez Jr. 22 Jan 1968 to 26 May 1991." The tanker was assigned to Fairchild AFB, Washington. (Campbell Archives/OKC)

NIGHTMARE from the 906th Air Refueling Squadron. (Amundson)

SWAMP WITCH (58-0061) from the 380th Bomb Wing at Plattsburg. (Campbell Archives/OKC)

KUKAI MARU is a KC-135 (59-1512) assigned to the 452nd Air Refueling Wing, Air Force Reserve at March AFB. She carries 54 camels indicating Desert Storm Missions. (Campbell Archives/OKC)

BUCCANEER (62-3515) is now a KC-135R with updated CFM-56 engines. (Campbell Archives/OKC)

SNUFFY'S TOY a KC-135R (63-7999) assigned to the 319th Bomb Wing at Grand Forks AFB, North Dakota. (Campbell Archives/OKC)

SNOW SHARK of the 906th Air Refueling Squadron on the Minot flightline, December 1, 1989. (Hill)

DREAM GIRL 2 on the ramp at Tinker AFB during a modification and update program. (Link)

60-0331 better known as WIND TRAVELER. (Campbell Archives/ OKC)

58-0057 sports Desert Storm mission markings along with a tribute to the 44th Bomb Group. (Campbell Archives/OKC)

MISS LINK an EC-135G served with the 28th Bomb Wing as an Airborne Launch Control aircraft. (Campbell Archives/OKC)

VIKING (62-3502) served with the 93rd Bomb Wing at Castle AFB, California. (Watton)

KC-135 (58-0091) PHOENIX from the 906th Air Refueling Squadron. She was involved in a minor mid-air bump with a B-52H in October 1987. (Amundson)

This nice artwork adorned the nose of KC-135E, 59-1489 from the 151st Air Refueling Group, Utah Air National Guard. (Campbell Archives/OKC)

A veteran of Operation Desert Storm KC-135 (59-1499) pays tribute to the POW-MIA. (Campbell Archives/OKC)

RODFATHER (63-8879) flew 28 mission from Turkey during Operation Desert Storm. She was assigned to the 906th Air Refueling Squadron at Minot. (Hill)

KC-10 GREAT WHITE (83-0077) was the 911th Air Refueling Squadron flagship. (Campbell Archives/OKC)

BLACK HILLS SENTINEL (86-0102). She was also known as LADYHAWK while serving with the 28th Bomb Wing. (Hill)

AMERICAN FLYER (86-0104) from the 28th Bomb Wing at Rapid City, South Dakota. (Rogers)

B-1B 86-0102 when she carried the noseart for LADY HAWK. (Rogers)

LONE WOLF (86-0106) carries the markings of the 28th Bomb Wing. This aircraft crashed in Texas on November 30, 1992 while assigned to the 96th Bomb Wing. (Rogers)

B-1B (86-0117) of the 319th Bomb Wing, Grand Forks AFB. She carried the name PRIDE OF NORTH DAKOTA and artwork to celebrate the state's Centennial Year 1989. (319th BW/PAO)

RUM RUNNER (62-3507) from the 340th Bomb Wing shows off her Desert Storm Scoreboard. (Campbell Archives/OKC)

KC-135 (62-3520) was known as BRUTUS to her crew chief, M/Sgt Elmer Amundson at Minot. (Amundson)

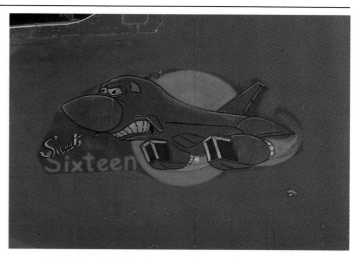

B-1B (84-0054) SWEET SIXTEEN from the 96th Bomb Wing at Dyess AFB, Texas. (Hill)

HUNTRESS (86-0103) of the 28th Bomb Wing makes an airshow appearance at Minot. (Hill)

B-1B (82-0001) LEADER OF THE FLEET from the 28th Bomb Wing. She was the first production B-1B. (Rogers)

GREMLIN of the 28th Bomb Wing. (Burridge)

B-1B (86-0121) carried the name AMERICAN MAID while serving with the 319th Bomb Wing at Grand Forks. (Hill)

SPECIAL DELIVERY (85-0066) from the 96th Bomb Wing, Dyess AFB, Texas. This was the second B-1B delivered to the 96th. She originally carried the name OLE PUSS. (Rogers)

DARK STAR (85-0083) from the 28th Bomb Wing, May 1989. (Rogers)

B-1B (85-0074) PENETRATOR from the 96th Bomb Wing. Her names refers to the B-1Bs capabilities. (Burridge)

ELDERSHIP was the first B-52G. After service in most B-52G equipped wings and combat over Viet Nam, she was retired on July 10, 1989. She now guards the main gate at Offutt AFB, Nebraska. (USAF)

An example of tail art carried by U-2 60-1098 from the 9th Strategic Recon Wing. (Burridge)

B-1B (86-0099) better know as GHOST RIDER. (Burridge)

B-52G (58-0257) FIRST STRIKE from the 42nd Bomb Wing. She flew combat during Operation Desert Storm. (Campbell Archives/OKC)

EL LOBO II From the 2nd Bomb Wing at Barksdale led the first low level mission flown by B-52s during the Gulf War. (Campbell Archives/OKC)

RUSHIN NIGHTMARE (59-2583) from the 416th Bomb Wing based at Griffis AFB, New York shows her off her Desert Storm scoreboard. (Campbell Archives/OKC)

B-52H (60-0035) SPECIAL DELIVERY on the ramp at Minot, on December 1, 1989. (Hill)

HIGH ROLLER from the 416th Bomb Wing. (Campbell Archives/OKC)

B-52D (56-0679) YELLOW ROSE was retired from the 7th Bomb Wing in 1982. (Campbell Archives/OKC)

B-52G (58-0164) from the 416th Bomb Wing flew combat missions during Desert Storm. Shown here on the ramp at Tinker AFB with some of her skin removed for modification and update. (Link)

KC-10 (87-0124) from the 4th Air Refueling Wing paid tribute to flight in the name THE SPIRIT OF KITTY HAWK. (Campbell Archives/OKC)

CITIES OF SHREVEPORT/BOSSIER; ROLLIN OUT THE RED. A KC-10 from Barksdale AFB. (Campbell Archives/OKC)

B-1B DAISEY MAE from the 96th Bomb Wing at Dyess AFB, Texas. (Campbell Archives/OKC)

Interesting nose art on KC-135E (56-3650) from the 157th Air Refueling Group of the New Hampshire Air National Guard. Only the men from the group really knew the significance of NUMBAH: FLUFFED & BUFFED BUZZARD. (Campbell Archives/OKC)

The F-85 Goblin was an experimental escort fighter to help SAC bombers reach the target. (Campbell Archives/OKC)

8
THE FINAL CUT

An F-85 approaches the B-29 mothership during hook up trials in the late 1940s. (Campbell Archives/OKC)

The F-85 has made the hook up and will soon begin the trip upward into the bomb bay. (Campbell Archives/OKC)

The F-85 Goblin fighter is snug in the bomb bay of the mothership as they head back to the base. (Campbell Archives/OKC)

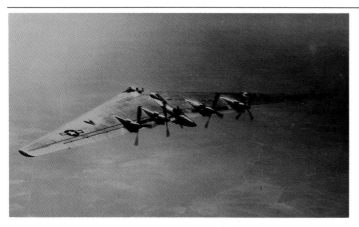

The XB-35 Flying Wing was a prime candidate for use by SAC as a heavy bomber. (Northrop/Pape)

The follow on to the XB-35 was the jet version YB-49. Both futuristic designs were beaten by politics, bad luck and the B-36. (Northrop/Pape)

The YB-60 was a jet powered version of the B-36. It flew on April 18, 1952. The YB-52 was over 100 miles per hour faster then the Convair aircraft. With that in mind, the YB-60 never had a chance to make SAC's bomber force. (Pape)

The SKYBOLT standoff missiles was to be shared by the United States and England. Cost overuns and a dubious test record caused the program to be canceled. (Ethell)

B-52G (57-6473) in her day-glo test paint carries a full load of four GAM-87A SKYBOLT stand off missiles. (USAF)

The XB-70 was supposed to be the supersonic follow on to the B-52. At Mach 3 speed, it could carry a payload over four thousand miles on internal fuel load. Here prototype (20001) flies high over the test range. (Campbell Archives/OKC)

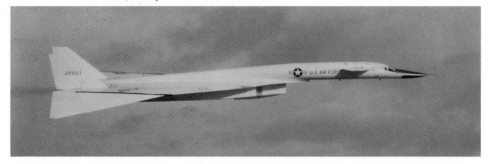

With her wing tips down the second XB-70 streaks across the skies in a Mach 3 speed run. (Author's Collection)

The first XB-70 made 83 flights before being retired to the Air Force Museum. (Author"s Collection)

B-1A (74-0160) was the third airframe built. Shown here complete with SAC sash and shield at Edwards AFB during testing. (Author's Collection)

B-1A (74-0174) in desert colors. President Carter canceled the project leaving nothing to replace the aging B-52 fleet. (Author's Collection)

Although the B-1A was canceled, it would rise again in the form of the B-1B. Shown here is the third B-1A on the Edwards ramp with equipment used to help keep the avionics cool in the desert heat. (Author's Collection)

The Northrop B-2 Stealth Bomber plugs into a tanker during refueling tests over the desert. (Northrop/Pape)

The B-2 resembles the earlier flying wings built by Northrop. That is where the similarity ends. Here a B-2 forms-up with a KC-135 tanker during testing. (Northrop/Pape)

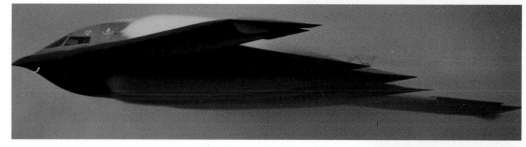

A B-2 pulls some interesting vortices in this photograph taken during a test. (Northrop/Pape)

Due to the increasing costs of the aircraft and the reduced need of a strategic bomber, the B-2 may well fly into history as the most expensive bomber never to reach operational status. (Northrop/Pape)

After her
service with
SAC this B-47
served with
the U.S. Navy
before being
preserved at
Pease AFB,
New Hamp-
shire.
(Burridge)

When Pease
AFB was
marked for
closure this
KC-97 was
dismantled
for removal to
another base.
(Burridge)

B-47 (51-
7071) CITY
OF ALTUS
served with
the 96th
Bomb Wing
at Altus
Oklahoma
before the
wing moved
to Dyess AFB,
Texas in
August 1971.
(Author's
Collection)

9
TIRED IRON

She served with the 7th, 42nd, 95th and 28th Bomb Wings. B-36J (52-2217) now resides at the SAC Museum near Omaha. (Hill)

One of two F-85 Goblins built for the parasite fighter program. This example is preserved at the SAC Museum. (Hill)

Most aircraft that are retired from the Air Force end up like these B-58 Hustlers. Basking under the Arizona sun these once proud bombers await the cutters axe. (Author's Collection)

A recent addition to the Strategic Air Command Museum at Offutt Air Force Base is this SR-71 Blackbird. (Hill)

C-119 Flying Boxcars were assigned to many SAC bases for support duties. This C-119 is displayed at Omaha's SAC Museum. (Hill)

This U-2C is preserved at Laughlin AFB, Texas. (Kerr)

U-2 (66-6701) is preserved at the SAC Museum, Offutt AFB. (Hill)

After serving as a test ship, flying combat and peacetime service with the 7th Bomb Wing, 55-0094 was retired to McConnell AFB, Kansas. (Author's Collection)

Little Rock AFB , Arkansas is the final home of B-47 52-0595. (Author's Collection)

The last B-47 to be retired from SAC served as a test ship. RB-47H (53-4296) has undergone a nose job and is preserved at Eglin AFB, Florida. (Author's Collection)

Since SAC used the C-124, it is only fitting that a example of "Old Shaky" be preserved at the SAC Museum. (Hill)

SAC used the T-29 for navigation training. Later they were used as staff transports. This example is preserved at the SAC Museum. (Hill)

Built by the Douglas Corporation, B-47E 52-1412 was retired from the 301st Bomb Wing to the SAC Museum. (Hill)

This B-47E (51-2837) sits on pylons at the Oklahoma State Fair grounds in Oklahoma City. (Campbell Archives/OKC)

This B-47 is displayed at Griffis AFB, New York. (Author's Collection)

This B-47 (53-4213) is preserved at Wichita, Kansas. (Author's Collection)

YRB-58 55-0666 painted to represent 61-2059 is displayed at Chanute AFB, Illinois. (USAF)

TB-58 55-0663 is displayed at Grissom AFB, Indiana. (USAF)

The ninth B-58 Hustler built (55-0668) was modified to a TB-58. She is preserved at the Southwest Aerospace Museum, Fort Worth, Texas. (Author's Collection)

On guard near the gate at Whiteman AFB, Missouri, is B-47E 51-2120. (USAF)

The second B-52B built (52-0005) is preserved at Lowery AFB, Colorado. (Carroll)

This KC-97 is preserved at March AFB, California. (S.D. Hill)

This B-29 is preserved at March AFB, California. (S.D. Hill)

KC-97 (53-0198) is preserved at the SAC Museum near Omaha. (Hill)

EB-47E (53-2135) last served with the 376th Bomb Wing. She is preserved at the Pima Air Museum. (Author's Collection)

B-47E 2275 wears the tail stripe of the 509th Bomb Wing. She resides at March AFB, California. (S.D. Hill)

The first B-52 to be delivered to the Strategic Air Command now resides at the SAC museum. (Hill)

Polished until she shines like new. B-58 Hustler 59-2458 has a home at the Air Force Museum at Dayton Ohio. (AFM)

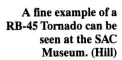

Resting in a place of honor at the SAC Museum is this C-54 that was used for staff transport duties. (Hill)

A fine example of a RB-45 Tornado can be seen at the SAC Museum. (Hill)

The YRF-84F Ficon prototype on display at the Air Force Museum, Dayton Ohio. (Moffitt)

SAC used the SA-16 for search and rescue. This example, complete with command sash is preserved at the SAC Museum. (Hill)

This SR-71 is on display at the Air Force Museum, Dayton Ohio. (Carroll)

This B-47 is preserved at the Museum of Flight, Seattle Washington. (Felling)

The last flyable B-47 taxis in at Castle AFB, California. The aircraft had been in storage at China Lake and made the last B-47 flight to Castle. (USAF)

After her last flight, B-47E 52-0166 was placed on display at the Castle AFB Museum. (Felling)

B-52D (55-0665) served in combat during Viet Nam. She came back with over 200 holes in her hide. She won her place of honor at the Air Force Museum. (Author's Collection)

When the new exhibit building was finished, old 665 was moved inside. She now rests with other historic aircraft out of the elements, preserved for future generations. (Carroll)

B-52D (55-0083) is preserved at Lowery AFB, Colorado. This was the second B-52 to score a MiG kill during Linebacker II. (Carroll)

B-52D (56-0695) served with the 7th Bomb Wing as her last unit. She was retired on October 5, 1983 and now resides at the Tinker AFB, Heritage Museum. (Hill)

B-52D (56-0679) flew combat in Viet Nam. She is preserved at March AFB, California. (S.D. Hill)

B-52D, 55-0071, CALAMITY JANE flew 38 missions over Viet Nam and later served with the 7th Bomb Wing. The tall tail BUFF is preserved at U.S.S. Alabama Memorial Park, Mobile Alabama. (Campbell)

A B-29 painted to represent the 96th Bomb Group from the 15th Air Force. The aircraft is preserved at March AFB, (Author's Collection)

This RB-36H is preserved at Chanute AFB. She served with the 5th, and 28th Recon Wings. There are a total of four B-36s preserved at various locations. (Felling)

B-58 (61-2080) was the last Hustler built. She was accepted by the 305th Bomb Wing on October 26, 1962. She is preserved at the Pima Air Museum, Tucson, Arizona. (Campbell Archives/OKC)

B-58 Hustler (61-2059) from the 305th Bomb Wing, set a speed record from London to Tokyo, under Operation Greased Lightning. The aircraft is preserved at the SAC Museum. (Hill)

B-47E, 53-2276, is preserved at the 8th Air Force Museum at Barksdale AFB. (Amundson)

This F-84F is preserved at Barksdale AFB. It wears the colors of the 27th Fighter Escort Wing. (S.D. Hill)

B-47 CITY OF ABILENE is preserved at Dyess AFB, Texas. (Harris)

After years of service, B-52G 58-9-2577 was retired. It now guards the highway near the main gate to Grand Forks AFB, North Dakota. (Hill)

A Minuteman missile transporter truck sits near the main gate at Grand Forks AFB. (Hill)

This Minuteman missile is preserved at Grand Forks. (Hill)

One of the few surviving examples of a Hound Dog stand off missile is preserved at Grand Forks. (Hill)

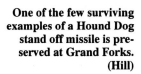

AFTERWORD
IN MEMORIUM

SAC CREWMEMBERS WHO DIED IN THE LINE OF DUTY

Abnoy, W.R., Maj
Abrogast, D.R, A1C
Achoy, J.M., TSgt
Acker, P.E., Capt
Ackley, C.D, 2Lt
Acklin, F., Maj
Adams, C., Capt
Adams, C.R., Capt
Adams, J.B., 2Lt
Adams, J.S., Capt
Adams, W.R., SSgt
Adcock, J.T., A2C
Addison, C.W., MSgt
Adler, G.E., SSgt
Adock, H.S., Maj
Adrean, P.B., Capt
Agard, L.H., Maj
Agenbroad, C., Lt Col
Agnew, R.P., Lt Col
Ahlgrim, H.G., A2C
Akermand, H.C., TSgt
Albasio, P.A., Capt
Albright, Y.P., MSgt
Alden, L.M., 1Lt
Aldridge, H.J., Capt
Alexander, D.E., 1Lt
Alexander, G.W., Maj
Alexander, H.L., TSgt
Alldredge, C.F., Capt
Allen, J.A., A3C
Allen, J.L., 2Lt
Allen, J.W., SSgt
Alley, B.A., Capt
Allison, D.R., 2Lt
Allison, R.V., Capt
Allred, C.B., A1C
Allsop, L.H., TSgt
Alston, D., A3C
Alston, R., A1C
Altamfrano, H., SSgt
Alworth, R.R., Maj
Ambrose, G.W., A1C
Amsden, R.D., SSgt
Anderlitch, R., 1Lt
Anderson, C.A., Maj
Anderson, J.J., 1Lt
Anderson, M.C., 1Lt
Anderson, P.F., Capt
Anderson, R., Maj
Anderson, R.C., Capt
Anderson, R.L., 1Lt
Andoe, E.J., Capt
Annis, T.R., A1C
Anolese, B.A., Maj
Apgar, W.J., Maj

Applebe B.E., Capt
Arambula, D., A1C
Archer, D.G., SSgt
Arend, J.S., Maj
Arger, D., 1Lt
Armom, R., 2Lt
Armond, R.L., Capt
Armstrong, J.R., TSgt
Armstrong, R.R., 2Lt
Armstrong, L.P., 1Lt
Arnold, D.R., SSgt
Arrand, D., Sgt
Arrington, P.E., TSgt
Arteaga, J.I., 1Lt
Asay, W.E., SSgt
Ascol, H., 1Lt
Ashe, R.A., Capt
Atherton, P., 1Lt
Atherton, F., Lt Col
Atherton, R.C., Capt
Auton, J., Gen
Avdevich, F.C., Capt
Avery, W.L., A1C
Aydoner, G., Capt
Aylers, H.S., SSgt

Baca, D.L., A2C
Bachman, D.C., 1Lt
Badowski, C.F., SSgt
Bagby, A.P., Capt
Bailey, J.O., Capt
Bailey, R.R., 2Lt
Bair, G.D., 2Lt
Baker, B.N., 1Lt
Baker, D.E., Maj
Baker, D.S., 1Lt
Baker, P.R., MSgt
Baker, J.W., A1C
Baker, L.D., SSgt
Baker, R.A., SSgt
Baker, W.S., Capt
Baker, W.W., MSgt
Balcer, S.C., SSgt
Baldwin, W.A., Capt
Baldy, P.J., Capt
Ballard, L.L., Maj
Ballard, W.L., A2C
Ballew, C.L., A1C
Banks, R., A2C
Banks, S.R., TSgt
Banrichtor, R.R., 1Lt
Barbor, Z.O., Lt Col
Barbour, A.L., TSgt
Barlett, R., Capt
Barlow, H.B., 1Lt

Barnah, P.W., A2C
Barnes, E.J., MSgt
Barnes, G.W., Capt
Barnes, J.R., 1Lt
Barnes, J.R., A2C
Barnes, W.E., A1C
Barnett, A.R., Capt
Barnett, L.N., Capt
Barney, L.E., SMSgt
Barnish, F.R., TSgt
Barr, B.V., 1Lt
Barr, R.H., Lt Col
Barry, H.L., Capt
Barry, H.P., 1Lt
Bartle, J.R., Maj
Basingor, L.C., Capt
Baska, R.S., 2Lt
Bass, J.C., MSgt
Bastin, M.R., Capt
Bausch, C.E., A1C
Bayer, F.E., 1Lt
Bayles, E., A1C
Bayon, R., A1C
Beach, D.L., Maj
Beale, G.W., Capt
Beam, A.P., Maj
Beam, R.B., A1C
Beam, T.L., Lt Col
Bean, R.M., 1Lt
Beard, A.L., A2C
Beard, J.V., SSgt
Beasley, H.G., Maj
Beattie, R.P., Capt
Boatty, C.H., Lt Col
Bechak, W.A., 2Lt
Beck, M.O., Maj
Beckman, R.W., 1Lt
Beezley, J.G., Lt Col
Bell, F.H., Maj
Bell, H.E., Capt
Bell, N.C., Col
Bell, R.S., Maj
Belleau, E., A1C
Bellotte, H.D., AB
Belt, J.E., 1Lt
Bemis, B.C., SSgt
Bence, F.E., TSgt
Benefiel, P.L., 1Lt
Benevides, E.G., TSgt
Benford, N.G., SMSgt
Benge, R.B., SMSgt
Bennett, H.L., A1C
Bennett, R.A., 2Lt
Bonnett, W.J., Maj
Bennett, W.R., Capt

Benton, C.E., MSgt
Berardi, J.D., 1Lt
Berenberg, D.A., AB
Berendzen, G.W., Capt
Berg, H.A., 1Lt
Berq, J.A., 1Lt
Bergdoll, W.M., Capt
Bergstrom, L.J., MSgt
Berliner, G.W., Capt
Berninger, W.C., Capt
Berquist, E.L., Col
Berry, F., A1C
Berry, W.L., Maj
Betsher, G.E., 1Lt
Bewley, H.H., 1Lt
Bexten, R.L. 2Lt
Beyer, B.P., Maj
Bieler, W.C., 1Lt
Biersdorff, C.F., A1C
Bill, J.R., TSgt
Binkley, L.L., A1C
Birch, R.L., Capt
Birdsell, P.L., A1C
Bischoff, D.L., A3C
Bise, D.F., TSgt
Bishop, D.P., 1Lt
Bishop, J.H., Capt
Bittenbender, D., Capt
Black, E., A1C
Black, G.W., Maj
Black, J.R., 1Lt
Black, R.B., 1Lt
Blackmore, B.R., Capt
Blackwell, J.V., SSgt
Blair, W.E., Capt
Blake, B.N., Sgt
Blakely, G.H., 1Lt
Blakes, B., SSgt
Blakeslee, R.F., Maj
Blankenship, C., Capt
Blankeship, C.D., 1Lt
Blazinga, R.E., TSgt
Blessing, C.D., 1Lt
Bloom, J., 1Lt
Bloomgren, R.D., 1Lt
Boedeker, W.C., SSgt
Boelter, E.W., 1Lt
Bohaty, A.R., TSgt
Bohling, R.L., SSgt
Bohn, B.J., A2C
Boland, J.E., Maj
Bolden, A.L., A2C
Boley, E.P., SSgt
Bolin, C.L., A1C
Bolstad, D.W., TSgt
Bolton, R.D., 1Lt
Bomberg, J.S., 1Lt
Bonin, H., Capt
Bonneville, H.S., Capt
Bonton, A.P., Capt
Boothby, G.B., Capt
Booy, W.F., 1Lt
Boozer, F.V., 1Lt
Bordwell, J.C., 1Lt
Bostich, C.D., Capt
Botten, A.J., SSgt
Bouchard, F.P., Capt
Boucher, R.L., Capt
Boutelle, C.A., 1Lt
Bovard, M.W., SSgt
Bowen, L.C., Capt
Bowles, W.P., 1Lt
Bowling, R., Capt
Bowman, H.V., Capt

Boyd, C.W., MSgt
Boyd, E.D., Capt
Boyd, F.Q., Capt
Boyd, H.W., A2C
Boyer, F.A., A3C
Bozeman, S., 1Lt
Brace, F.S., 1Lt
Bradbury, W.E., Maj
Bradley, W.S., TSgt
Bradshaw, F.F., MSgt
Brady, W.E., Maj
Branch, W.D., SSgt
Brandeberry, E., SSgt
Brandt, E.E., 1Lt
Bransdor, C.W., 1Lt
Brashear, F.D., Capt
Bratcher, D.H., Lt Col
Braunagel, L.F., 2Lt
Bray, D.J., A1C
Breackney, R.A., 1Lt
Breit, R., A2C
Brennan, W.J., Capt
Bretz, S.J., A1C
Brewer, J.L., MSgt
Bridges, E.A., 1Lt
Briggs, C.R., TSgt
Bristoll, B.C., SSgt
Bristow, J.M., 1Lt
Bristow, R.R., A1C
Brittain, G.F., Maj
Britton, W.A., Maj
Broadhead, L.J., 1Lt
Brock, P.E., 2Lt
Brock, J.R., Amn
Brockway, J.C., Capt
Broemmelsieh, B., Maj
Brontsas, G.M., Lt Col
Broods, B.A., Lt Col
Brookman, D.R., A2C
Brooks, A.J., SSgt
Brooks, A.L., Sgt
Brooks, R.N., Capt
Brose, K.E., SSgt
Brosius, C.W., Capt
Brovssard, J.D., A1C
Brown, A.K., Maj
Brown, C.E., 2Lt
Brown, C.W., Maj
Brown, D.C., 1Lt
Brown, F.L., MSgt
Brown, G.W., Maj
Brown, J.B., Maj
Brown, J.D., Capt
Brown, J.J., MSgt
Brown, L.R., A1C
Brown, L.R., Capt
Brown, R., A3C
Brown, R.A., A2C
Brown, R.R., A2C
Browning, J.W., 1Lt
Browning, R.M., MSgt
Brozowski, F.J., TSgt
Brugioni, R.J., TSgt
Brunnel, E.L., A1C
Bryan, J.H., SSgt
Bryan, R.G., 2Lt
Bryant, V.C., A2C
Bryne, C.B., Capt
Buchalew, H.J., 1Lt
Buchanan, M.O., Capt
Buehler, C.J., A3C
Bukovac, C.J., MSgt
Buley, W.A., MSgt
Burbank, C.A., Capt

Burch, C.A., Capt
Burch, L.F., Capt
Burdette, W., SSgt
Burgan, K.R., SSgt
Burges, J.M., A1C
Burgess, L.P., Capt
Burgess, W.S., 1Lt
Burke, C.F., A1C
Burke, W.L., Maj
Burmeister, A.L., Maj
Burnett, B.B., MSgt
Burnfin, J.J., A1C
Burns, R.D., 1Lt
Burris, C.H., MSgt
Burrows, W.H., A3C
Burt, F.W., Capt
Bush, E.R., Lt Col
Bush, W.G., 1Lt
Bushman, C.E., MSgt
Butler, B.E., SSgt
Butler, F.L., Lt Col
Butler, J.M., SSgt
Butler, P.P, TSgt
Butler, R.W., TSgt
Butts, C.J., Maj

Cable, R.C., Capt
Caibse, W., MSgt
Cairl, E.R., Maj
Calderon, S.B., 1Lt
Caldwell, R.C., A1C
Callegari, J.P., 1Lt
Calton, R.D., Capt
Cameron, D.C., TSgt
Cammack, B.E., Capt
Camp, J.B., Maj
Campbell, B.Y., A2C
Campbell, J.A., Capt
Campbell, L.M., Capt
Campbell, P., TSgt
Campbell, W.W., Capt
Campion, D.J., Maj
Cannata, C.J., A1C
Cannon, L.F., TSgt
Cannon, T.E., Capt
Cantrell, R.L., Capt
Cantu, F.R., A1C
Cantwell, R.P., Capt
Capitan, J.J., A2C
Capp, J.D., A1C
Cardinal, K., A3C
Cardoni, J.P., 1Lt
Carithers, C.E., 1Lt
Carlini, A., Lt Col
Carlisle, R.V., Capt
Carlow, C.P., 2Lt
Carlson, G.L., TSgt
Carlson, R.A., Maj
Carlson, R.W., 2Lt
Carmach, H.C., Lt Col
Carnes, W.A., Capt
Carpenter, P.S., Maj
Carrigan, R.C., Capt
Carriker, J.E., MSgt
Carrol, R., Capt
Carroll, J.L., 1Lt
Carter, J., 2Lt
Carter, J.B., Maj
Carter, M., SSgt
Carter, S., Capt
Casey, R.C., MSgt
Cashin, B.C., 1Lt
Cassie, R.G., 2Lt
Castle, L.R., Capt

Castleberry, S.L., Maj
Castor, D.G., 1Lt
Castrucci, A., TSgt
Catlin, J.C., Maj
Catrett, R., SSgt
Catto, W.A., Capt
Causey, W.T., 1Lt
Caye, E.J., 1Lt
Cervantes, M., Capt
Cervenk, H.W., 1Lt
Chamberlain, R., Capt
Chamberlain, W., Capt
Chambers, R.R., Maj
Champion, R.C., TSgt
Chandler, F.W., Maj
Chandler, W.S., Lt Col
Chapin, A.V., Capt
Chapla, F.J., Maj
Chaplain, R.J., SSgt
Chaplin, C.C., TSgt
Chapman, C., Capt
Chapo, R.J., 1Lt
Chase, R.E., Capt
Chatfield, R.W., 1Lt
Cherry, J.D., A1C
Cherry, J.D., SSgt
Chetneky, S.J., 1Lt
Child, W.L., A1C
Childress, H.W., SSgt
Childs, J.B., Capt
Childs, J.S., Maj
Chilton, J.R., SSgt
Ching, W.R.S., 1Lt
Chrisawn, F.S., 1Lt
Chrisides, A.V., A1C
Christ, R., SSgt
Christian, B.S., SSgt
Christian, L.V., 1Lt
Christopher, D.J., 1Lt
Chute, A.F., A2C
Ciereszewski, J., Sgt
Cincotta, R.P., 1Lt
Cinko, J., A2C
Cisneros, J., A1C
Clare, D.J., Capt
Clark, D.E., Capt
Clark, F.A., Maj
Clark, J.C., A3C
Clark, O.F., Capt
Clark, R.A., TSgt
Clark, W.R., MSgt
Clark R., A2C
Claunch, J.J., MSgt
Clausen, M.E., SSgt
Clausi, F.R., 1Lt
Claussen, G.A., 1Lt
Cleary, J.R., TSgt
Clemons, E.C., TSgt
Cloe, D.A., Sgt
Close, B.N., Maj
Coachman, B.P., Capt
Coates, R.E., 1Lt
Codington, R.E., 1Lt
Coffinger, E.J., A1C
Cohn, H.G., SSgt
Colandro, A.C., Capt
Cole, C.S., 1Lt
Cole, D.A., A1C
Cole, D.E., TSgt
Cole, L.E., Sgt
Coleman, B.L., SSgt
Colgan, S.A., SSgt
Collins, R.E., Maj
Collins, R.P., MSgt

Collins, W.C., 1Lt
Collins E.E., Capt
Colvin, W.A., SSgt
Combs, O.Q., TSgt
Commel, R.E., Capt
Connell, J.O., Capt
Connon, L.E., 1Lt
Consoluer, S.E., Sgt
Constable, R.A., Capt
Cook, F.N., A3C
Cook, J.E., A1C
Cook, O.C., 2Lt
Cook, V.J., Capt
Cooper, D.L., Maj
Cooper, E.J., A2C
Cooper, R.E., SSgt
Cootes, J.H., 2Lt
Copley, C.E., Capt
Cork, J.M., 1Lt
Corley, J.C., 1Lt
Corley, J.L., 1Lt
Cornett, M.W., Lt Col
Corsaro, L.M., 1Lt
Corvelli, D.D., 1Lt
Costello, R.P., TSgt
Cota, R.B., A1C
Cotterill, W., Lt Col
Cottle, F.E., SSgt
Couk, C.L., 1Lt
Counsell, J.R., Capt
Countess, S., A3C
Courcier, H.P., Capt
Cowart, C., MSgt
Cowart, E.H., Capt
Cowles, C.R., SSgt
Cox, E.O., 1Lt
Cox, H.C., A1C
Cox, K.W., 2Lt
Cox, M., SSgt
Coyne, J.H., Capt
Craft, L.J., Maj
Craigmyle, S.C., 1Lt
Craven, A., Capt
Craven, D.B., Maj
Cravens, J.W., 1Lt
Crayeraft, R.E., Capt
Crean, J.H., SSgt
Crecelius, C.E., Maj
Creech, W.C., SSgt
Crenshaw, R.E., 1Lt
Creo, A.B., Lt Col
Crews, A.B., Sgt
Critser, J.L., Capt
Crittenden, R.N., 2Lt
Crocker, A.B., MSgt
Crome, R.A., MSgt
Cromie, C.C., Capt
Crook, J.H., Maj
Cross, R.W., Capt
Crow, C.A., SSgt
Crow, J.R., A2C
Crowther, H.L., 1Lt
Crum, B.A., TSgt
Crumm, W.J., Maj Gen
Crump, D.O., Capt
Crump, E.R., Capt
Crump, H.W., Capt
Crump, H.W., SSgt
Crutchfield, W.B., Maj
Cubilla, P.J., SSgt
Culberson, W.G., 2Lt
Cullen, P.C., Gen
Cullen, W.E., A2C
Cunney, J.C., Capt

Cunningham, B., SMSgt
Cunningham, F.W., SSgt
Cunningham, M.R., Maj
Curtis, C., 2Lt
Curtis, D.E., SSgt
Curtis, F.R., Capt
Curtis, M.L., SSgt
Czvbowice, A., A1C

Dack, O.E., 2Lt
Dailey, C.P., A1C
Daly, J.N., Capt
Dames, W.F., Lt Col
Damico, M.F., Maj
Daniel, P.A., TSgt
Daniels, W., A1C
Dankey, R.G., Capt
Danos, A., A1C
Darby, R.B., SSgt
Darden, W.R., 1Lt
Darst, P.K., A3C
Daspit, E.J., Maj
Datel, A.F., A1C
Dauzvardis, F.G., Maj
Davenport, L.J., 1Lt
Davidson, J.C., A2C
Davidson, W.C., Capt
Davidson, W.H., Col
Davies, F.N., Capt
Davies, N.W., SSgt
Davignon, N.L., MSgt
Davis, C.J., TSgt
Davis, E.D., SSgt
Davis, E.K., SSgt
Davis, H.E., MSgt
Davis, H.R., Maj
Davis, J.R., Capt
Davis, J.T., Maj
Davis, P.E., Maj
Davis, R.A., A2C
Davis, S.S., Capt
Davison, R.E., Capt
Day, W.H., MSgt
Dean, B.D., MSgt
Dease, G.C., Lt Col
Deboer, H.L., 1Lt
Debonis, P.C., 1Lt
Decante, D.W., SSgt
Decatur, T.E., Maj
Decorleto, A.P., TSgt
Decota, T.J., SSgt
Deel, C.D., 1Lt
Deel, H.B., MSgt
Defrench, F.Y., 1Lt
Dejung, C.J., Capt
Dellinger, J.D., 2Lt
Delorme, G., 1Lt
Delpriore, D.S., SSgt
Dempsey, D.H., A1C
Denison, W.R., A2C
Dennie, W.R., A1C
Dennis, L.C., 1Lt
Dennis, R.C., Capt
Dent, J.F., Capt
Derby, R.E., TSgt
Devinney, III, SSgt
Devlin, W.R., SSgt
Devries, M.R., A1C
Dew, E.C., 1Lt
Dewitt, Q.L., SSgt
Dewolf, E.R., A2C
Dewolski, C.T., Capt
Dibble, J.C., 1Lt
Dickerson, D.F., 1Lt

Dickey, D.D., Capt
Dickson, W.E., TSgt
Diggle, B.W., TSgt
Dillenbeck, F., SSgt
Dillingham, H.E., SSgt
Dillon, J.E., 1Lt
Dingeldein, F.H., SSgt
Diobson, R.H., A3C
Dipierro, J., SSgt
Disanto, J.P., A2C
Dix, D.D., Sgt
Dixon, W.S., Maj
Dobbs, F.M., TSgt
Dobbs, M.L., Capt
Dolen, D.A., A2C
Donahue, D.F., MSgt
Donovan, P.B., Capt
Dooley, M.L., A1C
Dotts, R.L., 1Lt
Doughty, G.R., 1Lt
Doughty, R.H., Capt
Dow, H.R., 1Lt
Dowdy, R.E., Maj
Downs, V.B., SSgt
Doyle, G.E., Maj
Doyle, R.J., SSgt
Dozier, T.F., Capt
Drake, R., A2C
Dreher, C.F., TSgt
Dreher, C.S., TSgt
Drews, D.L., 1Lt
Dryer, J.A., 1Lt
Dubach, M.O., Capt
Dudek, M., Capt
Dudek, R., Sgt
Duffy, C.F., TSgt
Duggan, O.W., Capt
Dughman, G.D., SSgt
Dultmeier, G.A., Maj
Dunbar, E., A1C
Duncan, J.L., TSgt
Duncan, J.R., SSgt
Duncan, J.W., Capt
Dunham, J.R., 1Lt
Dunlap, M.F., Capt
Dyer, F.A., 1Lt
Dykes, L.M., Lt Col

Earharf, G.D., Capt
Earl, R.O., A2C
Earterling, J.W., Capt
Easton, D.S., 1Lt
Ecelbarger, P.R., Maj
Echstein, M., Capt
Eddleman, S.H., Capt
Edgar, C.W., A2C
Edgcomb, W.A., Maj
Edgell, A.L., SSgt
Edler, L.M., TSgt
Edmiston, G.T., MSgt
Edmonds, B.D., Maj
Edson, E.G., Capt
Edwards, R.J., Capt
Edwards, J.A., 1Lt
Edwards, J.R., SSgt
Edwards, M., A2C
Egan, J.P., 2Lt
Eggleston, G.V., 1Lt
Eggleston, R.P., 1Lt
Eifolla, J.P., Capt
Eisenhart, C., Maj Gen
Eland, J.J., A1C
Eley, C.W., Capt
Elke, H.F., SSgt

Ellington, H.W., 1Lt
Elliott, B.D., 1Lt
Elliott, R.S., Capt
Ellis, P.W., Col
Ellis, L.D., Capt
Ellis, R.H., SSgt
Ellsworth, R.E., Gen
Elonis, J.A., 1Lt
Emberton, H.C., SSgt
Emley, M.H., 1Lt
English, E.M., Capt
Ennis, E., TSgt
Ensor, N.H., Capt
Epling, W.E., 1Lt
Epps, E.W., 1Lt
Erks, R.S., SSgt
Esmond, T.M., Maj
Estep, E.B., TSgt
Estrada, J.P., 1Lt
Eubanks, J.D., Capt
Evans, A.L., SMSgt
Evans, E.A., 1Lt
Evans, E.G., Maj
Evans, H.R., Capt
Evans, J.W., Capt
Evans, R.R., SSgt
Everly, H.J., 2Lt
Ewing, F.E., Maj
Exell, W.L., A1C
Eyman, R.L., 1Lt

Fairbairn, D.W., Capt
Falconer, W.L., A2C
Fales, C.E., 1Lt
Falleh, R.W., 1Lt
Fallon, G.W., Lt Col
Fanhl, S.G., Capt
Fant, C.B., 1Lt
Fantel, J.M., Maj
Fantino, J.A., Capt
Farmer, R.E., 1Lt
Farmer, W.W., Capt
Farnsley, R.R., 1Lt
Farquahar, J.E., Capt
Faulconer, J.W., Capt
Faust, D.H., Capt
Fautech, R.G., 2Lt
Felix, D.W., Sgt
Fellows, P.D., 1Lt
Fendley, W.J., TSgt
Fenn, G.H., Capt
Ferguson, A.C., Capt
Ferguson, D.D., 1Lt
Ferguson, R.R., Capt
Ferguson, W.B., A3C
Ferguson, W.L., MSgt
Ferlazo, T.A., 1Lt
Fernandez, J., MSgt
Ferreira, W.F., Capt
Ferrell, J.D., A1C
Fessler, R.G., 1Lt
Fetterer, G.G., 1Lt
Fetterhoff, P.H., TSgt
Fetters, N.W., TSgt
Fewell, R.N., TSgt
Field, J.R., Capt
Fields, A.E., SSgt
Fields, R.W., TSgt
Fife, J.R., 1Lt
Filippoini, C.W., A3C
Finch, W.R., 2Lt
Findley, H.S., 1Lt
Finnegan, J.P., A2C
Finnell, D.O., A1C

Fischer, H.H., Capt
Fiser, L.E., Capt
Fish, R.L., TSgt
Fisher, E.O., Capt
Fisher, K.A., 1Lt
Fisher, P.R., Capt
Fisher, R.E., SSgt
Fisher, W.E., 2Lt
Fitzsimmons, V., TSgt
Flaitz, P.P., Capt
Flashch, J.A., 1Lt
Flater, D.L., Lt
Fleming, P.D., Col
Fleming, S.L., 1Lt
Flemming, J.C., SSgt
Fletcher, R.P., TSgt
Fletcher, T.O., A1C
Flick, G.S., Sgt
Floor, J.N., Lt Col
Flora, W.B., 1Lt
Florer, C.E., Maj
Flowers, H.L., 1Lt
Fogle, E.N., 1Lt
Fohl, W.F., SSgt
Fontana, C.P., 2Lt
Foote, G.M., 1Lt
Ford, C.H., MSgt
Forman, J.H., Capt
Forrester, B.W., Capt
Forster, M.W., Capt
Forsyth, D.A., TSgt
Foss, J.E., A1C
Foster, C.E., TSgt
Foster, D.F., Capt
Foster, D.L., Capt
Fowler, J.N., SSgt
Fox, R.H., SSgt
Fraher, O.V., Capt
Francis, R.V., Capt
Frankenberger, W., A2C
Franssen, C.M., A2C
Franz, H.O., SSgt
Frazier, E., SSgt
Frazier, J.S., A1C
Frazier, R.G., 1Lt
Fred, A.R., Capt
Frederickson, J., Capt
Freed, A.J., Capt
Freeman, R., MSgt
Friedman, L., 1Lt
Friend, L.V., 2Lt
Fritsche, R.A., 1Lt
Fritts, W.L., SSgt
Fritz, B.R., TSgt
Fritz, J., MSgt
Frommn, R.E., Capt
Fry, B.P., SSgt
Fryer, B.L., 1Lt
Fulbright, B.L., TSgt
Full, W.J., Capt
Fuller, W.G., Capt
Fulton, J.V., A2C
Fults, J.B., SSgt
Funk, K.M., Maj
Funnel, H.J., SSgt
Furda, J.S., 1Lt
Furnberq, C.C., A1C

Gabbard, D.H., MSgt
Gabree, D.W., SSgt
Gabriel, W.W., Maj
Gabriszeski, J., SSgt
Gaffner, G.L., Capt
Gafford, J.C., SSgt

Gaines, A.J., A1C
Galasso, W.A., MSgt
Galineau, J.M., A1C
Galvan, R.A., Capt
Gamache, G.P., Lt Col
Gardner, G.A., Capt
Gardner, R.C., A3C
Gardner, R.C., SSgt
Gardner, W.F., Maj
Garmer, A.J., 1Lt
Garnerm, N.W., A2C
Garret, W.W., A2C
Garrett, C.W., Maj
Garrington, J.F., 1Lt
Garrison, K.M., Lt Col
Gartner, G.A., SSgt
Gaskey, R.N., A1C
Gassett, W.E., 2Lt
Gassoway, G.J., A2C
Gastmyer, F.J.
Gatchel, C.W., Capt
Gaub, R.E., 1Lt
Gay, B.C., Maj
Gazell, E.G., 1Lt
Geghard, J., 2Lt
Gehrig, J.H., Maj
Gelino, H.E., A2C
Gemery, H., 1Lt
Gentry, B.C., Maj
George, R.L., Capt
Gerich, H., Lt Col
Gerlich, R.H., A1C
Gianahos, J.P., Capt
Giancola, C.D., AB
Gibbs, R.W., SSgt
Giberson, L., A2C
Gibson, C.A., SSgt
Gilbreath, A.L., SSgt
Giles, J.S., Capt
Gillard, J.E., 1Lt
Gillespie, J.W., 1Lt
Gillespie, S.O., Maj
Gillespie, W.E., Capt
Gilmer, B.M., TSgt
Gineros, P.J., Capt
Ginter, L.O., 1Lt
Gladdinq, D.R., 1Lt
Gladding, L.D., 1Lt
Glatz, W.E., 1Lt
Glaver, B.C., 1Lt
Glesner, G.J., 1Lt
Glover, R.B., 2Lt
Glyer, J.R., Lt Col
Goddard, J.A., Capt
Godfreg, G.O., A2C
Goffin, K.R., Capt
Goforth, O.C., Capt
Goggin, S.M., MSgt
Goggnen, R.F., A1C
Gomes, K.D., Capt
Gomez, P.P., A1C
Gonzalez, R.O., A2C
Goodal, P.A., Capt
Goodman, G.W., 1Lt
Goodroe, K.E., Capt
Goodwin, R., 1Lt
Goolsby, L.L., A1C
Gordon, J.B., Capt
Gordon, S.N., A2C
Gorman, R.E., Maj
Gorter, R., Capt
Gosney, C.A., 2Lt
Gould, J.L., A3C
Goulet, R.E., A1C

Goyette, K.T., SSgt
Grabb, A.C., SSgt
Graeber, J.H., Capt
Graham, J.E., 2Lt
Graham, H.E., Capt
Graham, W.P., A3C
Granja, E., A1C
Granquist, D., A2C
Grant, W.H., MSgt
Grau, L., SSgt
Gravaes, R.J., SSgt
Gray, D.D., 1Lt
Gray, D.E., Maj
Gray, H.E., SSgt
Gray, K.A., MSgt
Gray, K.N., Col
Gray, L.C., 1Lt
Gray, W.H., MSgt
Grebe, H.L., 1Lt
Grebowski, W.J., SSgt
Green, C.E., TSgt
Green, D.B., Capt
Green, H.O., Capt
Green, K.K., Capt
Green, T.P., SSgt
Green, W.L., Capt
Greenawalt, P.R., 1Lt
Greenberg, J., Capt
Greeson, J.R., 2Lt
Gregg, A.L., Capt
Gregg, H.L., SSgt
Gregory, N.C., MSgt
Gregory, W.P., Lt Col
Grey, H., TSgt
Grider, G.B., 1Lt
Grier, S., Capt
Griffen, J.R., Maj
Griffith, R.K., Sgt
Griffitts, G.D., 1Lt
Grigsby, S.C., Capt
Grogan, B.B., A2C
Grosick, P.D., A1C
Gross, G.G., A1C
Grosscup, J.J., 1Lt
Grover, J.A., TSgt
Gruenberg, E.D., A1C
Gudowski, F.G., Capt
Guerin, J.P., SSgt
Guest, J.H., A1C, 1Lt
Guiles, J.W., 1Lt
Gunn, L.A., TSgt
Gunther, C.D., Col
Gustavson, T.C., SSgt

Hackbarth, J.T., 1Lt
Hafendorfer, C., Capt
Hagan, F.L., 1Lt
Hagar, R.R., Maj
Haggard, R.L., Capt
Hagins, C.H., Capt
Hagood, L.H., Capt
Hale, D.R., 1Lt
Hale, L.P., MSgt
Halgren, R.L., A1C
Hall, G.H., 2Lt
Hall, P.M., Lt Col
Hallgarth, T.J., 1Lt
Hamilton, B.J., 21t
Hamilton, P.W., SMSgt
Hammons, J.J., Maj
Hampton, H.B., A2C
Hampton, H.E., MSgt
Hamry, G.N., MSgt
Hancock, J.P., A1C

Hanify, G.H., 1Lt
Hanna, H.H., A1C
Hansen, C.V., Sgt
Hansen, R.E., 1Lt
Hansen, H.J., MSgt
Hanson, H.L., Capt
Hanson, L.J., Capt
Harding, A.J., Capt
Harding, L.D., A1C
Hariton, D., Capt
Harkrader, G.G., 1Lt
Harlan, D.L., 1Lt
Harradine, Y.F., Capt
Harrell, R.C., A1C
Harriman, P.D., 1Lt
Harrington, E.R., Maj
Harris, A.W., A2C
Harris, B.C., Capt
Harris, J.C., Maj
Harris, H., A2C
Harris, R.B., Capt
Harrison, J.L., A1C
Harrison, L.E., SSgt
Harrod, C.L., MSgt
Harter, R.E., Capt
Hartley, J.R., Capt
Hartwell, O.W., SSgt
Harvey, J.H., 1Lt
Harvey, J.W., A1C
Harwell, S.A., TSgt
Haskell, L.H., Capt
Hatcher, L.F., Maj
Hauber, J., SSgt
Haugland, P.L., 1Lt
Hauser, H.C., Capt
Hawk, D.A., Capt
Hawley, D.C., Maj
Hay, T.D., SSgt
Hayden, C.J., 1Lt
Hayden, R.C., Capt
Hayes, J.J., 1Lt
Hayes, J.V., TSgt
Hayes, R.R., Capt
Hays, B., A1C
Hays, G.D., 1Lt
Hazlett, C.L., TSgt
Heaberlin, C.S., 1Lt
Heacock, J.L., A3C
Hearne, A.C., Lt Col
Heatherly, R.W., Capt
Heberling, F.R., 2Lt
Hebert, TSgt
Hedden, E.D., 1Lt
Hees, F.R., 1Lt
Heft, L.J., Lt Col
Heggem, P.O., 1Lt
Heiberf, D.W., Capt
Heil, P.L., 1Lt
Heiney, R.A., Maj
Held, C.W., Maj
Helmick, R.E., 1Lt
Hemm, V.F., Capt
Henderson, R.E., Capt
Hendrix, R.A., A2C
Henneke, N.O., 1Lt
Henry, C.A., Capt
Henry, F.B., Capt
Henss, F.A., Maj
Hepler, C.A., A2C
Hepstaff, E.B., A1C
Herbert, M.C., A2C
Herbold, J.M., Capt
Herrick, R.L., Capt
Herrick, P.B., Maj

Hertnecky, C.D., A2C
Hess, R.H., Capt
Hess, R.W., Maj
Hesse, C.W., A1C
Hewitt, M.C., TSgt
Hickman, R.D., Capt
Hicks, J.E., SSgt
Higginbotham, C., 1Lt
Higgins, D.J., SSgt
Higgins, W.A., Capt
High, H.C., 1Lt
Hilbert, W.J., 1Lt
Hiley, R.W., A1C
Hill, H.H., TSgt
Hill, R.J., Maj
Hill, W.R., MSgt
Hindman, J.E., A2C
Hinson, N.E., A2C
Hirsch, J.A., SSgt
Hirsch, J.B., Capt
Hixenbaugh, P.J., 1Lt
Hloucal, O.A., 1Lt
Hocker, R.A., Capt
Hodges, B.F., 1Lt
Hodgin, R.J., Capt
Hodgson, W.P., A3C
Hoffler, J.H., SSgt
Hogan, J.P., Col
Holder, J.C., SSgt
Holley, W.J., 1Lt
Holmes, J.J., SSgt
Holst, R.M., Capt
Holtz, A.J., 1Lt
Holub, H.E., 2Lt
Holzworth, D.H., 1Lt
Hooper, H.D., A2C
Hoose, T.C., Capt
Hopkins, H.J., Capt
Hopkins, J.J., Lt Col
Hoppe, H.J., A1C
Hoppens, R.E., A2C
Horine, S.M., A2C
Horn, L.A., 1Lt
Horn, O.R., AB
Horne, R.E., 2Lt
Horner, F.B., 1Lt
Hornsby, R., 1Lt
Hornsby, S.J., 1Lt
Horowitz, N.B., Capt
Horry, H.J., Capt
Horstman, W.C., Capt
Horton, C.B., TSgt
Howe, E.D., A1C
Howell, R.E., Capt
Hradisky, M.J., 2Lt
Hreha, G.R., SSgt
Huber, R.C., Capt
Huddleston, H.D., A1C
Hudelson, J.E., Maj
Hudson, J.W., Maj
Huffman, O.L., 1Lt
Huffmire, G.W., TSgt
Hughes, E.W, TSgt
Hughes, L.B., TSgt
Hughes, L.D., A1C
Hughes, S.R., Maj
Hughes, W.E., Maj
Hulshizer, A.J., Capt
Hummel, G.A., A3C
Humphrey, R., A2C
Hunsicker, R.W., Capt
Hunt, C.W., 1Lt
Hunt, J.S., Lt Col
Hunter, J.B., Maj

Hunter, J.P., 2Lt
Hunter, L.E., Capt
Hunter, R.K., A1C
Hunter, W.N., Capt
Hurdis, R.W., Lt Col
Huskey, W.F., 1Lt
Huston, P.W., SSgt
Hutter, J.G., TSgt
Hutto, T.C., 1Lt
Hutton, K.K., TSgt
Hyde, J.G., Capt
Hyman, H.E., MSgt

Imhoff, R.H., Maj
Ingham, G.H., Maj
Ingram, G., A2C
Insley, G.M., Capt
Ivey, R.G., A3C
Ivy, W.L., Col

Jack, D.D., MSgt
Jackley, G.A., 1Lt
Jackman, R.C., Capt
Jackson, C.R., SSgt
Jackson, D.W., TSgt
Jacobs, G.C., Capt
Jacobs, W., 1Lt
Jacobson, E., A1C
Jacox, W.W., 2Lt
Jacques, W.G., Maj
Jamerson, J.J., SSgt
James, R.L., A1C
Jannarone, F.P., 1Lt
Jarnot, J.J., 1Lt
Jarrett, J.P., Capt
Jellings, C.A., SSgt
Jenkins, A., A2C
Jenkins, J.W., SSgt
Jenkins, R.A., Capt
Jenkins, S.D., 1Lt
Jenner, J.L., 1Lt
Jennings, R.L., TSgt
Jenson, R.R., A2C
Jentsch, C.A., Capt
Jiles, J.C., Capt
Joaquin, A.P., 2Lt
Jobe, R.C., Maj
Jodoin, E., Maj
Johann, R., A2C
Johns, J.V., Maj
Johnson, A.K., Capt
Johnson, D.W., Capt
Johnson, E.R., 2Lt
Johnson, F.A., Capt
Johnson, F.B., Capt
Johnson, G.D., Capt
Johnson, H.G., Maj
Johnson, H.J., Capt
Johnson, J.L., Sgt
Johnson, J.W., 1Lt
Johnson, L.D., A3C
Johnson, L.V., Capt
Johnson, M.C., Maj
Johnson, R.A., SSgt
Jolicoevr, G.J., A2C
Jones, D.E., A1C
Jones, D.R., Sgt
Jones, F.B., A3C
Jones, F.J., SSgt
Jones, G.E., 1Lt
Jones, H., SSgt
Jones, H.P., TSgt
Jones, J.D.V., Capt
Jones, J.L., A2C

Jones, M.T., A2C
Jones, P., Capt
Jones, R., A1C
Jones, R.E., A1C
Jones, R.L., Capt
Jones, R.L., TSgt
Jones, T.G., A1C
Jones, W.A., SSgt
Joonas, J.B., A2C
Joseph, B.L., TSgt
Joyce, M.J., 1Lt
Joyce, T., Lt Col
Joyner, D.A., Lt Col
Judd, H.D., A2C
Jurzysta, T.S., Maj

Kaas, N.D., 1Lt
Kaeppler, R.B., 1Lt
Kahlmeyer, N.L., TSgt
Kaiser, M.W., Capt
Kalb, G.V., 1Lt
Kalberg, C., 2Lt
Kampert, R.F., Capt
Kamph, E.E., Capt
Kandetzki, A., 1Lt
Kane, L.R., A3C
Kapeles, J.H., 2Lt
Karlowitch, S.F., Capt
Karney, J.B., SSgt
Kaser, J.F., Capt
Kats, M.J., Capt
Kaylor, R.L., 1Lt
Kearney, J.L., 1Lt
Keel, B.E., Capt
Keith, J.B., Lt Col
Keith, T.G., 1Lt
Kelleher, J.F., Maj
Keller, D.L., Maj
Keller, J.S., 1Lt
Keller, M.B., 1Lt
Kelley, T.R., CApt
Kelly, F., 1Lt
Kelly, H.L., Maj
Kemp, H.D., 2Lt
Kemp, H.T., SSgt
Kendrick, F.G., A2C
Kenesnki, D.E., A1C
Kenny, D.A., 1Lt
Kenny, L.E., Capt
Kent, R.S., 1Lt
Kenyon, T.L., MSgt
Kern, J.W., 1Lt
Kernodle, B.L., Capt
Kerr, M.R., A3C
Kerri, G.R., A1C
Kerohner, B.H., A1C
Kesler, W.B., Lt Col
Ketchum, H.T., 1Lt
Kichler, S., Capt
Kilby, F.D., TSgt
King, G.W., A2C
King, B.T., 1Lt
King, R.L., A1C
King, R.T., 1Lt
King, T.W., MSgt
Kingman, D., Capt
Kingston, J.R., Capt
Kinzie, T.J., 1Lt
Kirby, P.E., SSgt
Kirk, J.W., 1Lt
Kish, S.L., MSgt
Kisonas, R.T., 2Lt
Kittle, L.L., 1Lt
Klaverkamp, B.J., A1C

Kline, T.M., 1Lt
Kline, T.S., 1Lt
Klinqenberg, R.D., 1Lt
Kloster, T.L., A1C
Knapp, L.F., SSgt
Knapp, T.J., TSgt
Knaub, J.J., 2Lt
Knight, P.W., A1C
Knight, T.B., A3C
Knight, T.R., TSgt
Knippa, A.J., Capt
Knippa, F.M., 2Lt
Knox, W.W., A2C
Knudsen, L.E., Capt
Knudtson, F.L., Maj
Kochimanis, T.T., 1Lt
Kolls, T.T., Capt
Koons, J.D., Capt
Kornegay, B.E., 1Lt
Koss, N.S., Capt
Kovar, R.J., 1Lt
Kowal, B.R., Capt
Kozel, F., Capt
Krah, C.P., MSgt
Kramer, E.V., Capt
Krauss, F.H., A1C
Krawier, T.N., Capt
Kriescher, J.T., A1C
Krohn, T.A., SSgt
Krull, V.R., Capt
Krumholz, B.J., A3C
Kub, E.A., 2Lt
Kuban, F.W., SSgt
Kudlak, J., TSgt
Kuehl, L.R., SSgt
Kueknel, D.D., 2Lt
Kuhn, K.A., 1Lt
Kurtz, R.L., 2Lt
Kuster, W.T., 1Lt
Kuzanek, J.K., Capt
Kuzik, T.J., A1C

Lachmund, R.E., Maj
Lack, S.D., 2Lt
Lacombe, B.A., Capt
Lacy, J.R., A2C
Lada, R., A2C
Lafleur, P.L., SSgt
Laine, L.F., TSgt
Laird, A., 1Lt
Lambiaso, R.E., Capt
Lammn, L.G., 1Lt
Landers, K.L., A1C
Lane, B.G., 1Lt
Lane, J.B., A1C
Lane, P.R., Capt
Laney, D.R., 1Lt
Langenberg, J.A., A1C
Langley, W.T., A2C
Lanois, B.D., Capt
Lapicca, J.B., A1C
Lapointe, M.A., Capt
Larivee, R.J., Capt
Larsen, S.B., 1Lt
Larson, A.P., 1Lt
Larson, R.A., Capt
Larson, T.G., 1Lt
Lassmann, L.D., Maj
Latimer, L.D., MSgt
Lauer, G.A., TSgt
Lawrence, D.G., SSgt
Lawson, W.J., Capt
Lea, L.L., TSgt
Leach, E.R., 1Lt

Leach, G.P., 1Lt
Leard, P.A., TSgt
Leblanc, J.E., A2C
Leclair, W.S., A2C
Ledbetter, L.B., MSgt
Lee, B., 1Lt
Lee, G.D., 2Lt
Lee, G.W., Capt
Lee, M.D., 2Lt
Leger, C.R., SSgt
Leggio, R.S., 1Lt
Leidolf, E.J., Maj
Lemming, J.L., Maj
Lemmon, W.B., Lt Col
Lemoine, E.J., SSgt
Lemons, E.M., MSgt
Lennep, T.C., Jr., 1Lt
Lenyua, N.A., SSgt
Lenzi, A.J., 1Lt
Lepage, L.S., TSgt
Lerose, L.J., 1Lt
Lett, W.R., Lt Col
Levine, F., 1Lt
Lew, L.R., TSgt
Lewch, R.L., A1C
Lewis, C.D., 2Lt
Lewis, D.R., 1Lt
Lewis, R.L., 1Lt
Leysath, J.C., 2Lt
Lichtenhan, R.F., Capt
Liebsach, C., SSgt
Lifzinger, J.W., Capt
Lighthall, R.R., A1C
Liles, J.M., MSgt
Limberg, G.H., 1Lt
Lincoln, R.F., Capt
Linder, F.T., 2Lt
Lindsey, R.L., SSgt
Link, P.H., Capt
Linn, C.E., A1C
Linton, G.B., SSgt
Lipina, R.H., A3C
Lisenbee, C.K., A3C
Liske, P.J., Capt
Littlefield, R.D., A1C
Lively, A.J., Capt
Livingston, D.L., SrA
Llewellyn, R.H., Capt
Lloyd, A.F., Maj
Lobell, A.Z., Capt
Lock, S.W., A3C
Lockemy, G.C., SSgt
Lockwood, J.H., 1Lt
Loncarovich, P., A1C
Longley, W.D., TSgt
Looch, J.W., 1Lt
Loontiens, J.D., A1C
Loper, W.W., A1C
Lotterer, D.A., Maj
Lovvorn, F.J., A3C
Lowe, R.G., Capt
Lowery, T.J., A1C
Lowry, T.G., Capt
Loy, D., SSgt
Luce, G.F., A2C
Luebke, R.J., Maj
Lumadve, J.L., SSgt
Lundberg, L.L., Capt
Lundy, H.E., 1Lt
Lungtrum, M.E., TSgt
Lunt, C.D., Capt
Luper, J.R., Col
Lush, W.J., TSgt
Lutjeans, S.P., Capt

Lyes, J.T., Capt
Lynch, W.F., A2C

Macchi, P.J., Capt
Mace, C.H., A1C
Macedonia, H.C., A1C
Machall, C.D., 1Lt
Maconi, J., SSgt
Madden, G.F., Capt
Maddos, T.A., SSgt
Maher, W.P., Capt
Maheux, P.J., SSgt
Mahler, P.V., Maj
Mains, J.A., A1C
Major, A.S., A1C
Mallon, G.J., SSgt
Malmstrom, F.A., Col
Malone, D.Y., A1C
Maltzberger, J., TSgt
Manassero, P., 1Lt
Mancos, P., A2C
Mangum, R.W., A1C
Manifold, R.P., 2Lt
Mann, F.J., MSgt
Mann, H.F., A2C
Manning, M.L., Maj
Mansfield, B.E., SSgt
Marcanti, A.C., 1Lt
Margocee, J., SSgt
Margolin, H.S., Maj
Marinich, A.J., Capt
Mariolis, T.N., A1C
Marker, B.T., Capt
Marks, A.P., TSgt
Marnon, W.B., SSgt
Marr, P.J., SSgt
Harsh, J.P., Capt
Marshall, H.T., 1Lt
Marshall, J.A., 1Lt
Marshall, L.J., Maj
Martel, R.N., Maj
Martin, H.E., 1Lt
Martin, H.T., SSgt
Martin, J.R., Capt
Martin, J.T., 1Lt
Martin, L.N., 2Lt
Martin, P.J., A1C
Martin, R.D., SSgt
Martin, R.B., Lt Col
Martin, R.J., 2Lt
Martin, R.M., Maj
Martin, W.E., MSgt
Martinez, E.J., A1C
Marting, R.L., A1C
Marx, E.A., Maj
Mason, M.J., Maj
Mason, R.L., TSgt
Mason, W.P., SSgt
Massie, J.B., Capt
Mateja, R.W., MSgt
Mathers, H.P., 2Lt
Mathews, O.L., Capt
Matson, A.H., Capt
Matthews, L.E., Capt
Matusewski, F.J., Capt
Mauck, F.G.D., Lt Col
Maxwell, W.T., Capt
Mayer, J.A., Capt
Mayfield, L.A., Capt
Maynard, R.T., Capt
McAdams, L.S., 1Lt
McAdams, O.T., MSgt
McAlister, J.F., TSgt
McArdle, J.J., TSgt

McBee, E.B., Capt
McCarron, J.E., 1Lt
McCarthy, A.E., 1Lt
McCartney, T.E., Capt
McCauley, J.R., SSgt
McCluro, G.A., Maj
McClure, J., SSgt
McClurg, R.H., 1Lt
McConegley, H.W., 1Lt
McConnico, T., Lt Col
McCoomb, L.E., Capt
McCormich, J.W., Maj
McCormich, R.T., 1Lt
McCormick, T.A., 1Lt
McCoy, H.L., 1Lt
McCoy, M.N., Col
McCoy, R.S., Capt
McCreedy, M.J., Capt
McCune, J.E., Capt
McCune, R.E., Maj
McDaniel, J.L., Capt
McDannell, J.E., 1Lt..
McDerby, T.B., Capt
McDermott, B., Capt
McDonald, R.N., Lt Col
McDonnell, W.A., SSgt
McDowell, J.T., A3C
McElwee, J.R., 2Lt
McEyer, H.W., Hnj
McFarland, SrA
McFlory, E., Capt
McGaffich, W.R., SSgt
McGee, R.D., A1C
McGregor, J.D., 1Lt
McGregor, J.L., Capt
McGregor, J.M, Capt
McGuire, W.J., TSgt
McGuirk, L.A., Maj
McHeage, G.R., SSgt
McHemey, G.R., Capt
McHeown, T.J., 1Lt
McHever, D.B., MSgt
McHillop, H.G., SSgt
McHugh, J.E., 1Lt
McIntosh, L., 2Lt
McIsaac, R.A., 1Lt
McKenna, B.J., Capt
McKenzie, J.T., 1Lt
McKinney, E.S., 1Lt
McKoy, E.A., Lt Col
McLaughlin, O.B., MSgt
McLennan, G.L., A2C
McMichael, R.E., 1Lt
McMillan, J.F., 1Lt
McMillian, W.P., Maj
McMullen, V.L., MSgt
McHullen, W.D., Capt
McNeil, G.E., A1C
McNeil, T.M., A2C
McPherson, P.M., Capt
McQuire, J.W., 1Lt
McVey, R.L., Maj
Meader, E.W., 1Lt
Meadows, W.A., Capt
Medland, J.L., A2C
Meekler, F.A., A1C
Meeks, N.V., Maj
Meinzen, R.W., 1Lt
Meissner, R.J., Maj
Melching, G.W., Maj
Mellinger, C.D., Maj
Menchhofer, L.G., 1Lt
Mendez-Peligrina, N., Capt
Mercer, J.A., Lt Col

Meredith, T.P., Sgt
Merman, H.D., 1Lt
Merrick, D.D., A1C
Merrifield, R.W., Capt
Merriman, R.T., TSgt
Merritt, R.W., MSgt
Merritt, T.J., A2C
Merva, S.J., SSgt
Messer, D.C., TSgt
Metcalf, J.R., Maj
Metz, J.A., Capt
Metzler, J.W., 1Lt
Michalac, S.S., SSgt
Michaud, C.B., Maj
Miching, T.E., Maj
Middaugh, B.D., 2Lt
Mignola, H.E., Lt Col
Mignosa, G.R., SSgt
Miles, R.V., A2C
Millar, E.G., Maj
Miller, A.H., Capt
Miller, C.D., Capt
Miller, C.H., A3C
Miller, G.H., Capt
Miller, J.E., 2Lt
Miller, R.A., TSgt
Milligan, A.M., Col
Milliken, C.W., A1C
Mills, B.L., Lt Col
Mills, M.C., Capt
Millspaugh, C.T., Maj
Miner, D.P., Maj
Miranda, L., A3C
Miskowski, E.A., Capt
Mitchell, J., 1Lt
Mitchell, J.A., A1C
Mitchell, J.J., 1Lt
Mitchell, R.C., Capt
Mitchell, R.R., A1C
Mitchem, P.M., Capt
Mittelstadt, L., Capt
Moberly, C.C., Capt
Moes, G.A., Capt
Moffatt, R.C., Col
Mohler, B.K., MSgt
Moncla, A.G., 1Lt
Montaneli, P.A., 1Lt
Montanus, S.S., 1Lt
Montgomery, O., MSgt
Montgomery, R., Lt Col
Moon, D.L., TSgt
Moore, A.R., SSgt
Moore, D.D., SSgt
Moore, D.W., A1C
Moore, H.E., A1C
Moore, L.S., TSgt
Moore, R.C., Capt
Moore, R.E., A1C
Morey, R.E., 1Lt
Morford, G.C., Maj
Morgan, B.E., Capt
Morgan, J.R., SSgt
Morganroth, R.N., Capt
Morin, H.S., TSgt
Moroney, E.J., Capt
Morrell, W.K., SSgt
Morris, D.C., Capt
Morris, R.J., Capt
Morris, J.H., A1C
Morris, W.T., Capt
Morrison, R.J., Maj
Morrissey, J.R., 1Lt
Morten, T.L., A3C
Morton, E.R., Capt

Mory, L.N., A1C
Mosby, J.W., 1Lt
Moses, E.F., Maj
Moss, A., SSgt
Moulton, T.F., 1Lt
Moultrie, T., 2Lt
Mountain, R.P., A2C
Moure, R.P., Capt
Mulheron, J.W., Maj
Mullan, J.M., 2Lt
Mullen, T.J., SSgt
Mullen, T.M., Maj
Muller, J.J., 1Lt
Mulligan, T.F., Maj
Mulvenna, S.M., A2C
Mumper, D.J., Capt
Murdock, R., 1Lt
Murphey, D.W., Capt
Murphy, D.J., SSgt
Murphy, E.E., Maj
Murphy, H.M., 1Lt
Murphy, T.P., 1Lt
Murphy, W.M., Capt
Murray, A.H., MSgt
Murray, D.A., A1C
Murray, F.L., A2C
Murray, J.F., Maj
Murray, R.M., Maj
Murry, T.J., 1Lt
Myers, G.W., SSgt
Myers, K.T., Maj
Myers, M.H., Capt
Myers, M.L., 1Lt
Myers, W.F., A2C
Myrick, E., SSgt
Myrick, J.L., Maj

Nadeau, T.E., Capt
Nall, R., A2C
Narramore, T.T., SSgt
Neail, F.E., A2C
Neely, T.A., Col
Neff, W.H., Capt
Negron, D.R., 1Lt
Neher, A.W., SrA
Neighbors, L.T., Capt
Neiss, J.V., A2C
Nellis, J.A., Capt
Nelms, H.L., TSgt
Nelson, A.E., Capt
Nelson, J.M., TSgt
Nemeth, R.W., TSgt
Neville, W.E., Capt
Neville, W.E., TSgt
Newick, A.F., 1Lt
Nichols, E.B., MSgt
Nichols, G.M., A1C
Nichols, J.D., SSgt
Nichols, L.E., 1Lt
Nicholson, W., 1Lt
Nicosia, R.J., Capt
Nida, R.T ., A1C
Nistifco, G.T., Maj
Noah, R.E ., SSgt
Noble, R.T., 1Lt
Noel, R.W., TSgt
Norris, M.B., SSgt
Norris, W.E., Maj
North, J.C., Capt
North, J.R., Maj
Northcutt, W.H., Capt
Norton, R.T., A1C
Noser, W.A., SSgt
Nowlin, L.W., Capt

Nunnelley, R.A., 1Lt
Nuscher, H.T., A2C
Nye, J.P., Capt

Odegard, J.V., SSgt
Odioren, G.B., 2Lt
Ogle, R.D., SSgt
Oherbloom, P., Lt Col
Oldham, T., 2Lt
Olds, J.D., A1C
Olear, M.S., 1Lt
Oliver, E.F., Capt
Olivo, R.T., A1C
Olsen, J., Capt
Olsen, W.F., A1C
Olson, A.B., A2C
Olson, J.J., Capt
Olsson, J.M., Capt
Olstein, J.L., Maj
Olvis, T.A., Sgt
Opoomer, T.H., 1Lt
Osgar, S., A2C
Ott, R.T., A2C
Ovorlees, L.E., SSgt
Ovorton, R.H., A2C
Owons, L.E., SSgt
Owingo, R.B., 1Lt
Oxehufwucl, N.D., Maj
O'Brien, B.A., Capt
O'Daniel, R.R., SSgt
O'Reefe, H.F., TSgt
O'Kelly, S.R., Capt
O'Leary, J.A., 1Lt
O'Toole, J.J., SSgt

Pace, J.E., 1Lt
Pace, M.L., Sgt
Pagelli, R.M., A2C
Palm, W.G., Maj
Pangrac, A., A2C
Pantilla, J.T., Capt
Pappe, J.A., Lt Col
Parham, R.L., A1C
Parish, R.E., A2C
Parkell, W.V., Maj
Parker, A.G., TSgt
Parker, J.F., A3C
Parker, J.R., Capt
Parker, L., Lt Col
Parkhill, D.A., 1Lt
Parson, H.L., SSgt
Parsons, A.T., Capt
Parten, K.H., Capt
Partridge, S.N., 1Lt
Pascal, P., Capt
Paszek, E.A., A1C
Patterson, F.E., 1Lt
Patterson, R.R., A1C
Patterson, O.T., 1Lt
Pattiaon, T.B., 1Lt
Patton, J.F., Col
Patton, T.H., 1Lt
Paul, C.A., Capt
Paul, D.G., A2C
Pauley, T.J, SSgt
Paull, W.T., Capt
Pauls, T.O., SSgt
Paulson, W.L., Capt
Paulson, R.A., 1Lt
Payn, N.W., Capt
Payne, K.L., 1Lt
Payne, R.L., Maj
Payne, W.N., Capt
Payton, W.H., TSgt

Pazin, P., Capt
Pearce, A.F., A2C
Pechskamp, R.T., Capt
Peebles, T.N., Maj
Pemberton, R.W., TSgt
Pennington, P.J., 1Lt
Perdue, M.J., Capt
Perkins, W.H., Maj
Perky, J.D., Capt
Perry, J.B., A1C
Perry, S.L., Capt
Petek, J.L., 2Lt
Peter, T.V., Maj
Peters, J.L., 1Lt
Peterson, R.A., A1C
Peterson, N.D., 1Lt
Peterson, R.H., SSgt
Peterson, T.V., TSgt
Peterson, W.T., Capt
Pettner, D.L., A3C
Petty, D.S., 1Lt
Petty, J.G., 1Lt
Phelps, D.A., Capt
Phillips, D.B., Capt
Phillips, J., Capt
Phillips, T.E., 1Lt
Phillips, W.M., Capt
Pickett, R.T., TSgt
Pickett, T.W., TSgt
Pickrell, H.A., SSgt
Pierson, J.S., Maj
Pinz, T.N., Capt
Piskula, R., TSgt
Pittman, L.E., Capt
Pizzeck, G.J., Capt
Platt, J.J., 1Lt
Platt, R.L., Capt
Pleaaon, H.J., 2Lt
Plog, R.T., Capt
Plonski, W.A., TSgt
Plough, D.J., TSgt
Plucker, D.D., 1Lt
Pogue, T.A., A2C
Pollard, E.W., SSgt
Polliam, T.T., Lt Col
Pomeroy, J.B., A1C
Poole, C.D., Lt Col
Poole, J.M., Capt
Poole, H.D., Lt Col
Poole, T.E., 1Lt
Pooser, E.T., 1Lt
Poppoff, N.M., SSgt
Porter, T., Capt
Porterfield, S.G., Col
Portis, K.O., 1Lt
Posa, E.E., Maj
Post, L., 1Lt
Posvenchuck, N., A3C
Potolicchio, L., MSgt
Potter, L., MSgt
Potter, T.M., Capt
Pounders, A.P., 1Lt
Powell, G.M., SSgt
Powell, J.A., 1Lt
Powell, R.T., SSgt
Powell, T.E., MSgt
Powers, T.A., Sgt
Powers, W.J., A3C
Poytress, E.F., Capt
Prachniac, J., SSgt
Prallow, L.M., 1Lt
Premedsky, R.M., Capt
Prestoch, H.P., MSgt
Price, D.J., Capt

Price, W.A., Maj
Priddy, H.D., SSgt
Pridgeon, J.L., A1C
Priecko, J.P., 1Lt
Primm, W.A., 1Lt
Primrose, R.L., Maj
Prinkey, R.E., SSgt
Pritchard, W.H., Capt
Pritchett, W.E., 1Lt
Procknal, E.S., Capt
Profilet, R.T., 1Lt
Proslevich, J., A1C
Provenzand, V., A2C
Pruett, J.B., Capt
Pudwill, P.L., Capt
Pulliam, J.R., Capt
Pump, H.T., 1Lt
Puque, J.D., 1Lt
Pylant, J.B., SSgt

Quam, B.A., Capt
Quandt, J.J., Maj
Quigley, J.H., SSgt
Quinn, K.A., TSgt

Raby, L.P., A1C
Racioppo, C., 1Lt
Rackley, J.R., A1C
Rae, W.R., A2C
Rafferty, L., 1Lt
Rafferty, L.E., Capt
Rainer, T.C., SSgt
Ramasocky, J.R., A1C
Ramisch, M.J., Capt
Ramone, C.J., Capt
Ramsdell, R.G., 2Lt
Ranck, L.B., 1Lt
Rapp, W.L., Capt
Rappaport, L.M., Maj
Rasmussen, D.B., Capt
Rasmussen, H.J., 1Lt
Rasmusen, J.A., 1Lt
Rasor, F.J., Lt Col
Ratagick, W.F., MSgt
Rathbun, C.S., Col
Ratke, D.C., A3C
Rav, H., Capt
Rawlings, O.D., Capt
Ray, J.P., Capt
Ray, M.D., A1C
Rea, F., MSgt
Reardon, M.B., TSgt
Reasor, T.W., Capt
Rebmann, M.R., 1Lt
Reddig, J.B., Capt
Redmond, J.H., A1C
Reece, R.C., Maj
Reed, W.H., TSgt
Reeter, R.R., Capt
Reeve, L.A., A3C
Regan, W.J., Capt
Regele, W.D., 1Lt
Reid, G., Capt
Reid, J.H., 1Lt
Reid, L.E., 1Lt
Reiley, G.M., 1Lt
Reilley, J.M., TSgt
Remy, N.J., A2C
Renner, R.N., Maj
Renner, S.D., SSgt
Reynolds, D.C., A3C
Reynolds, D.J., Capt
Rial, R.M., 1Lt
Richards, E.B., Maj

Richards, N.O., Capt
Richards, R.A., Maj
Richards, W.L., 1Lt
Richardson, C.W., Capt
Richardson, G.D., Capt
Richardson, J.B., Capt
Richardson, R.E., A2C
Richardson, R.P., 1Lt
Ridlon, R.A., AB
Riffle, C.W., Capt
Riggs, R.B., TSgt
Riley, G.E., TSgt
Riley, O.C., MSgt
Rinebold, B.L., Capt
Ringwall, R.W., 1Lt
Rissi, D.L., Lt Col
Ritter, L.J., Capt
Roach, R.P., Capt
Roark, R.B., SSgt
Robarts, R.E., 2Lt
Roberts, C.W., Capt
Roberts, H.J., MSgt
Roberts, T.S., Lt Col
Roberts, W.M., MSgt
Robertson, C.E., Capt
Robertson, J.C., Capt
Robinson, A.P., SSgt
Robinoon, C.G., Lt Col
Robinson, J.P., Capt
Robinson, O., Capt
Roche, G.R., Capt
Rochello, B.H., A2C
Rockotto, W.P., SSgt
Rockholt, W.P., SSgt
Rodgers, B.H., 1Lt
Roeglos, W.S., 1Lt
Rogers, D.N., Capt
Rogers, L.E., MSgt
Rogers, M., A1C
Rogers, H.H., A2C
Rogers, O.F., Lt Col
Rolfe, G.H., Lt Col
Roman, L.J., A2C
Rominiecki, L.A., Sgt
Roquot, W.D., TSgt
Rose, J., SSgt
Roseman, S.R., Capt
Rosencragce, R., SSgt
Rosenzweig, H., Capt
Rosetti, R., 1Lt
Ross, C.W., A1C
Rousher, R.D., SSgt
Rousseau, D.P., Maj
Rowland, W.A., 1Lt
Rowley, K.R., 1Lt
Roybal, T.Q., SSgt
Ruble, R.E., TSgt
Ruch, C.W., A1C
Rudolph, G.B., 2Lt
Rune, N.W., TSgt
Ruohonen, K.R., A3C
Rusk, M.P., SSgt
Rusk, V.H., Capt
Russell, B.S., 1Lt
Russell, C.J., A2C
Russell, R.Y., A2C
Russell, T.P., Maj
Russell, W.G., Capt
Ruzicka, J.L., Capt
Ryan, E.W., 1Lt
Ryan, J.E., SSgt
Ryan, R.W., Capt

Sager, L.A., TSgt

Sakry, J.P., Maj
Salavarria, E.M., Maj
Salazar, T.C., SSgt
Salinas, A.D., 1Lt
Salley, D.A., 1Lt
Sanderson, W.J., 1Lt
Sansom, H.B., SSgt
Sarchet, A.H., 2Lt
Saunders, D.W., Gen
Savoca, W.C., Capt
Sawyer, H.H., Capt
Sawyers, L.G., 1Lt
Sayre, J.H., 1Lt
Scalia, R.S., A1C
Scarbough, E.D., MSgt
Schaefer, B.E., A1C
Schafer, J.P., SSgt
Schardong, J.G., Maj
Schartz, D.J., 1Lt
Schatz, L.J., TSgt
Schell, R.R., SSgt
Scherier, T.F., Capt
Scheriff, A.T., 1Lt
Schlacter, W.E., 1Lt
Schmaling, M.R., Capt
Schmidt, F.D., MSgt
Schmidt, J., TSgt
Schmidt, L., 2Lt
Schmidt, R.E., Capt
Schneider, R.E., SSgt
Schock, P.E., TSgt
Schorr, J.L., A2C
Schultzaberger, G., A1C
Schulz, G.W., SSgt
Schulze, H.V., SSgt
Schuver, H.J., A2C
Schwab, V.R., 1Lt
Schwank, D.J., SSgt
Schwartz, D.P., Maj
Schwartz, U.N., MSgt
Schwee, C.W., Capt
Scoff, S.O., Capt
Scott, E.D., Capt
Scott, J.N., SSgt
Scott, R., A1C
Scott, W.L., SSgt
Scroggins, D.R., SSgt
Scserback, J.H., A2C
Seckman, J.K., Capt
Seegers, J.F., 1Lt
Sefton, J.L., Capt
Segalla, C.L., Capt
Selleck, E.R., 1Lt
Selleg, K.S., MSgt
Sellers, R., A3C
Sells, T.P., A2C
Selmo, M., 1Lt
Semple, D., Capt
Seng, L.F., SSgt
Servetas, E., Maj
Seymour, W.G., TSgt
Shaffer, B.L., A2C
Shames, B.M., A1C
Sharp, E.W., Maj
Sharrock, W.L., 1Lt
Shelton, E., Maj
Shepherd, F.L., SSgt
Shepherd, N.G., 1Lt
Sherman, R.L., Maj
Sherwood, F.E., Capt
Sherwood, L.D., Maj
Shields, E.F., Capt
Shields, S.H., A2C
Shingler, H.J., Col

Shipka, E.F., Capt
Shipman, J.E., Capt
Shipp, T.G., A1C
Shira, M.H., 1Lt
Shirk, F.R., Capt
Shook, K.W., A1C
Short, G.W., SSgt
Short, R.H., 1Lt
Shuller, E.P., 1Lt
Shultzbgr, G.A., A1C
Shumard, B.D., Capt
Siling, A., Capt
Sillier, A., A3C
Silvestri, F., A2C
Simmons, L.E., Capt
Simonfy, J.M., Maj
Simpson, C.G., Capt
Simpson, J.B., A2C
Simpson, J.R., Lt Col
Sinclair, H.L., A3C
Singleton, J.M., Sgt
Sipes, J.L., Capt
Sisco, J.A., TSgt
Sitra, C.J., A2C
Skidmore, R.D., Capt
Skiff, M.F., Capt
Skipworth, B.L., Col
Slaggle, C.T., SSgt
Slaughter, K.W., 1Lt
Slifkey, C.G., SSgt
Smith, C.P., 1Lt
Smith, D.C., 1Lt
Smith, D.D., 1Lt
Smith, D.W., A1C
Smith, E.E., SSgt
Smith, E.J., Capt
Smith, P.B., Capt
Smith, F.G., A1C
Smith, P.S., MSgt
Smith, G.C., MSgt
Smith, H.G., Capt
Smith, H.L., 1Lt
Smith, J.W., 1Lt
Smith, L.V., TSgt
Smith, M.B., 1Lt
Smith, O.Z., SSgt
Smith, R.C., Lt Col
Smith, R.D., SrA
Smith, R.E., 1Lt
Smith, R.V., Capt
Smith, W.A., Maj
Smith, W.C., 1Lt
Smith, W.E., 1Lt
Smithwick, R.N., Capt
Smokovitz, W.J., 1Lt
Smullins, G.R., Capt
Snead, A.J., SSgt
Snodgrass, W.F., AB
Snow, J.L., Maj
Snow, R.H., Capt
Snow, R.H., SSgt
Snyder, J.N., SSgt
Snyder, O.W., Capt
Snyder, R.P., TSgt
Soderbeck, E.G., Capt
Solis, M.A., A1C
Solt, R.H., 1Lt
Sorenson, G.L., MSgt
Soroe, G.F., A1C
Souza, M.M., 1Lt
Sowinski, E.R., 1Lt
Spangler, J.N., 1Lt
Spencer, L.R., SSgt
Spencer, M., 1Lt

Spencer, W.R., Capt
Spicer, H.S., 1Lt
Spiller, H.H., Maj
Spivey, W.E., A1C
Sporling, R.D., A3C
Sprague, G.D., 1Lt
Springer, E., TSgt
Sproat, R.L., AB
Squier, E.B., Capt
Stafanski, E.L., Maj
Stahl, A.J., 1Lt
Stalling, M.E., 1Lt
Stalmach, T.H., 1Lt
Stalmaker, R.E., 1Lt
Stanko, J.G., MSgt
Stannard, R.M., 1Lt
Stanton, V., SSgt
Staples, D.E., Maj
Starke, R.C., Capt
Starley, W.S., 1Lt
Stavb, H.H, 1Lt
Stear, A.W., SSgt
Steel, B.B., Maj
Steen, R.J., SSgt
Stein, E.H., Capt
Steinman, A.L., SSgt
Stenehiem, O.L., Capt
Stephenson, R.H., 1Lt
Sterling, A.W., SSgt
Sterling, H.E., Capt
Sterling, J.C., 1Lt
Stern, L.R., Capt
Stevens, C.W., Capt
Stevens, J.L., TSgt
Stewart, A.C., 1Lt
Stewart, B.B., A3C
Stewart, D.W., 1Lt
Stewart, H.C., Capt
Stimpson, C.E., SSgt
Stine, F.J., Capt
Stinnett, T.J., SSgt
Stoddard, G.H., Maj
Stoddard, R.W., Maj
Stoffell, L.E., MSgt
Stone, B.W., 1Lt
Stone, M.S., Capt
Stonesifer, C.H., Capt
Storey, A.B., 1Lt
Stout, F.L., MSgt
Stovall, W.E., A1C
Stowers, B.J., Capt
Stradford, T.G., A2C
Straley, N.A., SSgt
Strassheim, R.A., A3C
Stratton, J.H., Capt
Stratton, R.A., A2C
Strine, P.E., Maj
Stroud, H.A., Capt
Stuart, C.E., SSgt
Stubblebine, H.A., 1Lt
Stubblefield, W., TSgt
Stuber, S.E., Maj
Stuff, V.D., Maj
Stultz, T.J., 1Lt
Styles, H.S., 1Lt
St. George, R.L., 1Lt
St. John, R.E., 1Lt
Suitenko, L., Capt
Suiter, F.W., 1Lt
Sullivan, A.W., 2Lt
Sullivan, H.H., STU
Sullivan, J.J., Capt
Sullivan, J.P., WO
Sullivan, J.W., Capt

Summerall, J.D., A3C
Sumner, D.F., Maj
Sundberg, G.R., 1Lt
Sussillo, N.B., Capt
Sutton, D.F., A2C
Sutton, D.T., 1Lt
Sutton, T.E., Capt
Svelmoe, R.G., 1Lt
Swanson, J.E., A1C
Swearingen, G.V., Capt
Sweet, J.C., 1Lt
Swim, V.P., Capt
Swisher, C.G., A2C
Swisher, J.H., 1Lt
Sykora, C.E., A1C
Szabo, G.J., Maj
Szmuc, C., Capt
Szufer, S.J., 2Lt

Tabler, R.T., Capt
Taff, A.B., 2Lt
Taliaferro, D., TSgt
Tallmadge, T., Capt
Tallone, G.E., Capt
Tannor, E.E., A3C
Tanner, L.P., Capt
Tapp, M.L., SSgt
Tardie, J., SSgt
Tatum, J.E., 1Lt
Tatum, R.P., A1C
Taulbee, C.R., A2C
Taylor, J.E., Capt
Taylor, J.F., A2C
Taylor, L.G., A1C
Taylor, H.D., 2Lt
Taylor, P.A., 2Lt
Taylor, R.D., 1Lt
Taylor, R.G., TSgt
Taylor, W.W., Capt
Teetor, R.J., Capt
Tejeda, P.J., Maj
Tellerday, J.E., 1Lt
Tellier, R., 1Lt
Temple, E., Capt
Templeton, R., Maj
Tennille, J.M., SSgt
Tennyson, V.R., A1C
Teragawachi, K.R., 2Lt
Terry, L.A., SSgt
Testerman, R.E., 1Lt
Tewart, J.S., Capt
Tharpe, C.M., 1Lt
Theis, J.M., MSgt
Theis, L.A., Capt
Theriot, D.R., A2C
Thevret, B.G., TSgt
Thiel, V.G., 1Lt
Thomann, T.C., Capt
Thomas, B.G., A2C
Thomas, H., Capt
Thomas, J., Col
Thomas, J.W., Maj
Thomas, N.E., SSgt
Thomas, R.J., 1Lt
Thomas, R.J., SSgt
Thomas, W.A., 1Lt
Thomas, W.E., Maj
Thomas, W.W., Lt Col
Thomason, A.L., 1Lt
Thomason, P.E., SSgt
Thompson, D.R., 1Lt
Thompson, E.R., SSgt
Thompson, J.E., 2Lt
Thompson, J.T., TSgt

Thompson, L.E., SSgt
Thompson, R.L., Capt
Thorin, L.A., Capt
Thrush, M.B., A2C
Tibbetts, C.E., TSgt
Tibbetts, R.H., 1Lt
Tichenor, J.H., Maj
Tillman, G.E., 1Lt
Tilton, E.O., Capt
Tilton, F.A., SSgt
Timmens, W.O., SSgt
Tingwald, H.F., SSgt
Tisik, H., 1Lt
Toalson, A.J., 1Lt
Toffel, G.J., 1Lt
Tomesek, F.J., 1Lt
Tomlinson, W.J., 1Lt
Tooker, C.A., 1Lt
Toomey, F.W., 1Lt
Tornigal, B.L., 1Lt
Toups, P.G., Capt
Towe, H., MSgt
Towers, L.F., 1Lt
Towle, R.E., SSgt
Townley, R.E., Maj
Townsend, J., MSgt
Trapp, J.A., Capt
Travis, J.A., SSgt
Travis, R.P., Gen
Trawick, C.M., 1Lt
Tremblay, L.D., Lt Col
Trepanier, A.S., 1Lt
Trevisani, J., Lt Col
Trickey, F.L., Lt Col
Trochak, F.L., Lt Col
Troshynski, T.L., A2C
Trost, H., Maj
Troutman, J.M., TSgt
Troyer, C.E., A1C
Troyer, R., SSgt
Tubbs, C.D., Lt Col
Tucker, J.L., A3C
Tucker, O.B., 1Lt
Tuninello, R.T., 1Lt
Turner, G.P., A3C
Turner, J.E., Capt
Turner, J.M., Capt
Turner, J.P., A3C
Turner, L.F., 1Lt
Turney, G.D., A1C

Ullom, R.E., SSgt
Ulrich, J., TSgt
Umshield, M.T., A1C
Unger, J., Capt
Upp, D.A., 1Lt
Urban, R.T., A1C
Urban, W.F., A1C
Urquhart, R.L., Maj

Vail, J.J., SMSgt
Vainisi, J.J., 1Lt
Valavan, H.L., Capt
Valentino, W.J., Capt
Vana, R.P., SSgt
Vander, K.J., TSgt
Vandereyk, R.J., A2C
Vandermullen, R., 1Lt
Vanderpool, R.D., A1C
Vanderslice, T., TSgt
Vangilder, T.H., MSgt
Vanleuven, T.O., A2C
Vanpatten, K.E., SSgt
Varney, K., SSgt

Vasey, E.F., A1C
Vasquez, E., A1C
Vass, B.N., Capt
Vaughan, A.E., 2Lt
Vaughan, J.D., 1Lt
Vaughan, J.L., Lt Col
Vaughn, B.J., A1C
Vaughn, P.R., 1Lt
Veasey, M.A., Maj
Veck, M.M., Capt
Veers, R.W., Capt
Velazquez, F., Capt
Venskus, A.F., Capt
Ventimiglia, C.N., Maj
Verbo, D.A., AB
Vereen, H.V., TSgt
Vessel, L.E., Capt
Vickers, D.A., SSgt
Vied, J., TSgt
Vigil, R., SSgt
Vincent, R.S., Capt
Visconte, G.R., SSgt
Vitt, R.J., Capt
Vonblond, P.A., Capt
Vrabec, P.A., TSgt
Vulich, J.B., A1C

Wagamon, A.W., Capt
Waggoner, T.H., Capt
Wagner, D.J., A3C
Wagner, K.A., Maj
Wagner, W.A., Capt
Wagoner, G.C., Capt
Wakeland, J.O., Capt
Walder, W.P., SSgt
Waldrep, T.T., SSgt
Walkemeyer, W.F., 1Lt
Walker, A.G., Capt
Walker, C.A., Capt
Walker, E., SSgt
Walker, H.A., Capt
Wall, A.W., 1Lt
Walla, G.J., Capt
Wallace, G.E., SSgt
Wallace, K.E., 1Lt
Wallace, R.L., SSgt
Wallace, W.R., 1Lt
Waller, J.W., A1C
Walsh, W.B., Capt
Wandel, D.M., Sgt
Ward, C.W., 1Lt
Ward, J.C., Capt
Ware, J.V., SSgt
Ware, J.W., A3C
Warner, E.L., Maj
Warren, E.T., SSgt
Warren, G.W., A2C
Warren, R.H., Capt
Was, P., Capt
Waste, R.J., Maj
Waters, P.D., TSgt
Waters, H.E., 1Lt
Watkins, R.E., Capt
Watson, E.P., Capt
Watson, J.H., Capt
Watson, R.S., Lt Col
Wawrzyniak, A.A., Capt
Weatherwax, J.J., Capt
Weaver, E.J., Capt
Weaver, J.E., Capt
Weaver, R.T., 1Lt
Webster, N.R., 1Lt
Weeks, H.T., Lt Col
Wegner, R.S., Capt

Weinman, R.C., Capt
Weise, C.F., 1Lt
Welborn, R.D., 1Lt
Welch, J.E., Capt
Welch, R.M., 1Lt
Weller, T.T., Capt
Wellman W.F., 1Lt
Wells, E.R., Capt
Wenstrup, P.R., Capt
Went, R.R., SSgt
Werkheriser, W.O., A1C
West, N.P., A1C
West, R.C., Capt
West, R.E., SSgt
Westerhouse, P., Capt
Westrup, R.L., 1Lt
Wetherbee, J.A., 1Lt
Wetzel, R., 1Lt
Wewe, M.E., A1C
Wheeler, F.G., Lt Col
Whipple, R.R., 1Lt
Whiston, D.F., 2Lt
White, J.R., Capt
White, M.F., Capt
White, S.E., SSgt
White, V.T., 1Lt
Whitley, J.Y., Capt
Whitlock, J.B., A2C
Whitlock, T.A., Capt
Whitlock, W.D., Maj
Whitmore, D.A., Maj
Whitney, G.E., Capt
Whyte, F.R., Maj
Wicksell, R.C., 1Lt
Widek, H.L., TSgt
Widseth, G.J., Capt
Wieso, R.B., 1Lt
Wiggins, L.C., 1Lt
Wight, H.E., Capt
Wigley, W., 2Lt
Wikstrom, R.H., Capt
Wilbanko, C.R., A1C
Wilford, J.L., Maj
Wilhelm, F.E., Capt
Wiliams, A., SSgt
Wilkie, R.O., 2Lt
Wilkie, T.A., 1Lt
Wilkinson, C.L., 1Lt
Will, J.O., Maj
William, D.C., 1Lt
Williams, C.A., A1C
Williams, E.Y., Capt
Williams, J.G., Capt
Williams, J.L., Lt Col
Williams, N.S., Capt
Williams, R.C., SSgt
Williams, R.D., 1Lt
Williamson, F.C., A2C
Williamson, H.C., MSgt
Williamson, R.H., 2Lt
Willis, J.R., SSgt
Willis, R.O., A2C
Wilson, C., Col
Wilson, D.V., A1C
Wilson, E.C., TSgt
Wilson, G.G., Sgt
Wilson, J.R., 1Lt
Wilson, R.E., A1C
Wilson, R.B., Maj
Wilson, W.H., 1Lt
Wimbrow, N.J., Capt
Winegardner, J., MSgt
Winfield, N.E., SSgt
Wirt, J.H., Maj

Wise, R.V., MSgt
Witkowski, R.L., Capt
Witt, R.S., Capt
Witzes, R.R., Capt
Wojtowicz, J., MSgt
Wolf, D.L., A2C
Wolf, D.W., Lt Col
Wolfendale, C., Lt Col
Womack, J.O., Capt
Womble, L.E., TSgt
Wonders, D.F., TSgt
Wood, B.G., A1C
Wood, L.D., TSgt
Woodall, J.J., A1C
Woodard, L.B., MSgt
Woods, J.E., A2C
Woods, S.E., SSgt
Woods, W.G., Lt Col
Woodward, D.C., 1Lt
Woody, R.B., Maj
Woolbright, Lt Col
Wooten, H.D., TSgt
Workman, H.B., 1Lt
Would, W.J., Lt Col
Wovries, C.E., SSgt
Wren, P.T., 1Lt
Wright, B.R., Capt
Wright, F.C., Maj
Wright, G.T., Maj
Wright, K.B., Capt
Wright, L.E., A1C
Wright, T.L., Sgt
Wright, W.D., Capt
Wright, W.G., TSgt
Wrinckle, E.R., Maj
Wurtsmith, P.B., Gen
Wyatt, E.W., Capt
Wyatt, W.E., Capt
Wykert, R.G., 2Lt
Wyman, F.H., Lt Col
Wynn, D.D., Lt Col
Wynne, B.J., A1C
Wynne, E.L., A2C

Yeingst, J.A., Capt
Yeronick, S.H., Capt
Yoeman, R.E., SSgt
Yoke, D.J., A2C
Yon, O.W., Capt
York, J.R., 1Lt
Youman, W.L., Capt
Young, C.R., 1Lt
Young, C.R., Maj
Young, G., Maj
Young, H.E., MSgt
Young, J., 1Lt
Young, R.A., A1C
Yuvan, J.A., A1C

Zabawa, E.D., Capt
Zalac, F.B., Capt
Zalonka, C.C., Capt
Zayac, G.M., A2C
Zebedes, J.A.A., MSgt
Zemaitis, J.C., 1Lt
Zepp, R.E., Col
Zettle, B.B., Capt
Ziegler, G.W., Capt
Zielinski, E.T., 1Lt
Zoeller, H.O., Capt
Zumba, P.G., Capt
Zuppan, L., Maj
Zurivitza, W., Capt
Zweugartt, K.C., Capt

Strategic Air Command Memorial Window
SAC Memorial Chapel
Offutt Air Force Base, Nebraska